The Princeton Review®

W9-BRW-265

CRASH COURSE
for the GMAT®

4th Edition

by Cathryn Still
and the Staff of The Princeton Review

PrincetonReview.com

Penguin
Random
House

The Princeton Review
24 Prime Parkway, Suite 201
Natick, MA 01760
E-mail: editorialsupport@review.com

Published in the United States by
Penguin Random House LLC, New York,
and in Canada by Random House of
Canada, a division of Penguin Random
House Ltd., Toronto.

ISBN: 978-1-101-88166-8
eBook ISBN: 978-1-101-88172-9
ISSN: 1546-0355

Editor: Meave Shelton
Production Editor: Kathy G. Carter
Production Artist: Craig Patches

Printed in the United States of America on
partially recycled paper.

10 9 8 7 6 5 4 3 2 1

Fourth Edition

Editorial
Rob Franek, Senior VP, Publisher
Casey Cornelius, VP Content Development
Mary Beth Garrick, Director of Production
Selena Coppock, Managing Editor
Meave Shelton, Senior Editor
Colleen Day, Editor
Aaron Riccio, Editor
Orion McBean, Editorial Assistant

Random House Publishing Team
Tom Russell, Publisher
Alison Stoltzfus, Publishing Manager
Melinda Ackell, Associate Managing Editor
Ellen Reed, Production Manager
Kristin Lindner, Production Supervisor
Andrea Lau, Designer

Acknowledgments

Our GMAT course is much more than clever techniques and powerful computer score reports; the reason our results are great is that our teachers care so much about their students. Thanks to all the teachers who have made the GMAT course so successful, but in particular the core group of teachers and development people who helped get it off the ground: Alicia Ernst, Tom Meltzer, Paul Foglino, John Sheehan, Mark Sawula, Nell Goddin, Teresa Connelly, Phillip Yee, Kimberly Beth Hollingsworth, Bobby Hood, Chris Chimera, Chris Hinkle, Peter Hanink, and Cathy Evins.

Special thanks to John Fulmer, National Content Director for GMAT, and Kyle Fox for their hard work revising the current edition.

Special thanks to Adam Robinson, who conceived of and perfected the Joe Bloggs approach to standardized tests and many of the other successful techniques used by The Princeton Review.

About the Author

Cathryn Still received a bachelor's degree from Trinity University and a master's from The University of Texas. She joined The Princeton Review in 1990, starting as a teacher, and ultimately moved into management, where she served as Managing Director of Graduate Programs from 1997 to 2000.

Contents

PART I

Introduction

Orientation

What Is a Crash Course?

So the GMAT is coming up fast, and all your best intentions of studying an hour a day for the past three months have gone out the window. Not to worry—there's still hope. *Crash Course for the GMAT* will give you an effective strategy for tackling the GMAT, even though you're down to the wire. After a brief overview of the format of the entire GMAT, we'll dive right into a ten-step study plan designed to give you the highest possible rate of return. We've broken down each section by question type, and identified the best strategy for each type of question you'll see on the exam. But *Crash Course for the GMAT* is not a comprehensive study guide for the GMAT—if you have more time and that's what you're looking for, try The Princeton Review's *Cracking the GMAT.*

What Is the GMAT?

The Graduate Management Admissions Test (GMAT) is primarily intended to measure the aptitude of applicants to Masters of Business Administration programs. The test is not an indicator of intelligence, nor will it in any way predict your grades in business school or the likelihood that you'll sell your start-up for $50 million three years out. It's just a measure of how well you perform on standardized tests.

The GMAT is made up of three parts:

1. An Analytical Writing Assessment (AWA)
2. An Integrated Reasoning section
3. A multiple-choice section with two parts, Verbal and Quantitative (Math)

Analytical Writing Assessment

The Analytical Writing Assessment (AWA) is a 30-minute section during which you must develop an essay. The essay, called an Analysis of an Argument, requires you to critique the position of an author on a particular dilemma or argument. The test creators have developed a simple word-processing program that allows you to compose your essay on the computer screen.

Integrated Reasoning Section

The 30-minute Integrated Reasoning section consists of 12 items, each of which has multiple parts. Items may contain charts or tables and may ask you to evaluate information from different sources. Most questions feel like math questions, but a few may also test your verbal abilities. The Integrated Reasoning section has four types of questions. The four types of questions are as follows:

- Table Analysis
- Graphics Interpretation
- Multi-Source Reasoning
- Two-Part Analysis

Multiple-Choice Section

The multiple-choice section of the GMAT has two subsections, Verbal and Quantitative (Math).

The 75-minute Verbal section consists of 41 multiple-choice questions, approximately 25 percent of which are experimental (not scored). We'll tell you more about the experimental questions later. In this section, you'll see three types of questions (in no particular order):

- Reading comprehension (approximately 13 questions and 4 passages)
- Sentence correction (approximately 17 questions)
- Logical reasoning (approximately 11 questions)

The 75-minute Quantitative section of the GMAT contains 37 questions, approximately 25 percent of which are experimental (not scored). There are two types of questions (again, in no particular order):

- Problem solving (18–22 questions)
- Data sufficiency (15–19 questions)

Who Writes the GMAT?

The GMAT is owned and sponsored by the Graduate Management Admission Council (GMAC), a nonprofit organization with a board composed of top administrators and deans who set the standards for admission to accredited business schools in the United States. The test itself is produced by ACT Inc. (which creates the ACT and develops test questions for a wide variety of standardized tests) and by Pearson Vue, which distributes the exam to testing centers around the country.

How's It Scored?

Your GMAT scores will be broken down into three separate scores, one for the AWA, one for the Integrated Reasoning section, and one for the multiple-choice section of the test. The AWA essay is graded holistically on a scale of 0 (unintelligible) to 6 (well done).

The Integrated Reasoning section is scored from 1 to 8 in 1-point increments. Questions have multiple parts, and you must answer each part correctly to get credit for the question. The Integrated Reasoning score is not included in the Overall score.

Your performance on each multiple-choice section of the test generates a two-digit number, called the sectional subscore, ranging from 0 to 60. These subscores are combined into a three-digit number, called your composite, or overall, score. Overall scores range from 200 to 800. The average (50th percentile) GMAT score is around 550, while a score of 710 would be above the 90th percentile. A 700 is currently the 89th percentile.

Scores on the AWA, Integrated Reasoning, and multiple-choice portions of the exam are separate—they do not affect each other in any way.

Experimental Questions

Scattered throughout the Verbal and Quantitative sections of the test are questions that do not count toward your score. These are experimental, or research, questions, and their sole purpose is to generate data for GMAC. You will not recognize the experimental questions; they look and feel just like the real things. GMAC uses your performance on these questions to determine their viability and to generate scoring statistics for them.

What Do You Guys Know, Anyway?

The Princeton Review has been monitoring the GMAT for years. Our teaching methods were developed—and are continually honed—through regular, detailed analyses of *what* topics are tested on the GMAT and *how* these topics are tested. We teach strategies that allow you to quickly discern the most efficient and safest path to take in answering questions, and techniques that help you take control of the testing structure and environment, and even use them to your advantage.

How to Register

The GMAT is given, by appointment only, in computer testing centers. While theoretically you could call at any time and arrange to take the test the next day (the GMAT is administered nearly every day of the month), it's best to call well ahead of the day you wish to sit for the test. During peak times (October through March), testing appointments may fill several weeks in advance.

You can take the GMAT year-round, on almost any day, and as of this writing, it will cost you $250. You can take the GMAT once every 31 calendar days and a maximum of five times in a year. The easiest way to register is online at GMAC's GMAT website, www.mba.com.

There you can also find information on all sorts of topics, including the following:

- The latest GMAT information, including upcoming MBA forums
- Practice test questions
- Analytical Writing Assessment (AWA) essay topics
- Testing sites and phone numbers
- Links to hundreds of business schools
- Financial aid information

While your score for the multiple-choice section is available almost immediately after taking the test, business schools require you to file an official score report, which is typically released by GMAC two to four weeks later. Make sure you are scheduling your GMAT test far enough ahead of your application deadlines for your schools to receive your official scores.

Computer Adaptive? What on Earth Does That Mean?

In the GMAT, the multiple-choice Quantitative and Verbal sections are computer-adaptive tests (CATs). In a CAT, the order of the questions is not determined in advance. Each new question you see is determined by your performance on the question that preceded it.

The Integrated Reasoning section, on the other hand, is a linear section. The order and the difficulty of the questions you see are determined in advance.

What Will the Test Look Like?

Your GMAT will start out with an untimed tutorial in which you'll learn how to use a mouse, how to scroll, how to type your AWA, and what the various icons that appear throughout the test mean. Once you have completed the tutorial, you'll take your AWA. Then, after a short break, your multiple-choice test begins with the Integrated Reasoning section.

Each section begins with an instruction screen for the type of question you are about to see. These instruction screens are timed, so don't spend any time reading them—you'll know all you need to know about them by the time you finish this book.

Real Tests

Although this book will give you the practice and basic skills you need to take the GMAT, it's a good idea to fine-tune your techniques by testing yourself with some real questions written by the test writers, ACT. You can get a good idea of how a GMAT feels by using GMAC's *GMATPrep* software, which includes real GMAT questions presented in computer-adaptive mode. You can also take a practice GMAT on our website, PrincetonReview.com. For additional practice questions, consider using GMAC's *The Official Guide for GMAT® Review,* which includes more than 800 released questions. Both *GMATPrep* and *The Official Guide for GMAT® Review* are available through www.mba.com, the same site where you register to take the GMAT.

Disclaimer

At the time this book went to press, the information in it was current. You can find the most up-to-date information about the GMAT by consulting GMAC's website, www.mba.com, or our website, PrincetonReview.com.

General Strategy

How Adaptive Testing Works

Instead of subtracting the total number of incorrect answers from the total number of questions, computer-adaptive testing calculates your score progressively. Here's how it works: When you start each multiple-choice section of your GMAT, the computer knows nothing about you, so it estimates your score to be average, right in the middle of the scale. The first question you'll see in each section of the test is likewise a question of average difficulty, one that roughly 50 percent of test takers answers correctly. As you proceed through the test, the computer revises its assessment of you, both by giving you questions that are more or less difficult (depending on your answers), and by adjusting its estimate of your score up and down, until it has enough information to assign you a subscore for that section. Your subscores are then simply added and converted to your composite score.

How to Make It Work for You

The computer weighs your performance on earlier questions more heavily than it does later ones. Early in the test, your score will move up and down (hopefully, up!) in large increments, but as you near the end, your score will change only by small amounts. With this in mind, you can use the structure of the test to your advantage.

Take a look at this diagram, which shows the performance of two test takers in the first five minutes of their respective tests.

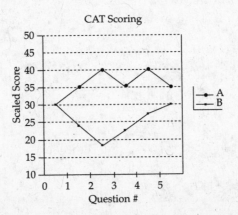

Crash Course for the GMAT

Test taker A starts off well. She gets the first question right, and the computer's estimate of her score increases accordingly. The second question is more difficult, but she gets it right, too, and her score increases again. The third question is slightly more difficult than the previous two, and gives her some trouble. She gets it wrong, so her score drops. The fourth question, then, is a little easier, and she gets it right so her score goes back up. She misses the fifth question and the computer, at this point, estimates that her subscore is about 35.

Now look at the line for test taker B. He misses the first two questions and his subscore plummets. He gets the third, fourth, and fifth questions right, but the computer estimates his subscore after five questions to be about five points lower than that of test taker A, even though both missed two out of five. The moral of the story: Earlier questions are more important than later questions.

Therefore, you should spend a little more of your time on early questions, ensuring that you get those right, than on later questions. You can make up the time by answering the later questions, which don't affect your score as much, more quickly. However, every question is important so don't slow down too much on the early questions. A good rule of thumb is to spend no more than three minutes answering any one question.

Remember that the questions are multiple choice, so the right answer is there, somewhere. But sometimes the challenge is not so much to identify the right answer, as it is to identify the four wrong ones. This brings us to our first technique, Process of Elimination (POE). By using POE you can improve your score on the GMAT.

Process of Elimination (POE)

Let's say you're faced with a sentence correction question you know contains an error, but you can't identify it. Since you can't skip the question, you'll have to guess, right? And if you guessed blindly, you'd have a 1 in 5 chance of getting it right. But let's say that by reading carefully through the answer choices, you can identify even one wrong answer and eliminate it. Then your chances of guessing correctly improve to 1 in 4. If you can eliminate two answers, your chances jump to 1 in 3. As you continue using Process of

Elimination, you could even eliminate all the incorrect answers and get the question right, but at the very least you'll improve your chances of guessing correctly.

Many of the wrong answers on the GMAT are created in hopes of trapping a test taker who solved the question by conventional means but made a careless but predictable error. There's always an answer waiting for these folks, appearing to be right when it isn't. By using POE to eliminate wrong answers instead of trying to divine the right one, you're less likely to fall into those traps.

Choose What's Left

We'll say one more thing about POE and the four wrong answers. After you've eliminated four that definitely have something wrong with them, the answer you're left with may not fill you with joy. It may not seem right even after you've eliminated four that were less right. Don't fret—just go with it. Keep this in mind as you're working through POE. Don't eliminate an answer simply because you don't like it. That answer may still be the credited response.

Answer Every Question

You must answer every question on the GMAT, because you can't proceed to the next question without answering the one you're on. If you fail to answer every question in a section (even if the last few are guesses), you'll be penalized. How? The computer will take the score it calculated for you up to that point, and reduce it by roughly the percentage of the test that you've left unfinished. If you leave $\frac{1}{4}$ of the questions unanswered, the computer will reduce your score by 25 percent. Ouch! So do your best to record an answer for every question, even if you have to guess.

Watch the Clock

In the upper right corner of the computer screen, you will see the time that remains in your section. When only five minutes remain, that's your signal to start wrapping it up. Quickly assess how close you are to the end, and accelerate your pace so you record an answer for every question.

Use Your Noteboards

Since all of the questions appear on a computer screen, you will not have a test booklet in which to write. However, you will receive a booklet of yellow noteboards to use as scratch paper. The noteboards are basically laminated card stock. They are the size of a sheet of legal paper and have a fine grid on them like that of a piece of graph paper. You will receive five of them, spiral bound at the top into a booklet. You will write on them with a fine-tip marker. To achieve your best results on the GMAT, you must use the noteboards.

For starters, you'll use your noteboards to keep track of Process of Elimination. It does no good to eliminate an answer choice if you keep reconsidering it. Therefore, you should *cross out* each answer choice as you eliminate it, but you can't cross it out on your computer screen. That's where your noteboards come in.

On the GMAT, each answer choice has a bubble next to it, but in this book we'll refer to the choices as (A), (B), (C), (D), and (E). Each time you see a question, get into the habit of immediately writing down A, B, C, D, and E on one of your noteboards. By doing so, you're less likely to lose your place or become confused. As you work through each question, you can eliminate those pesky wrong answers choices by crossing out their letters on your noteboard. As you're crossing them out, it will become more evident which one is the best answer. When you're finished with a question, draw a line under your work before starting the next question. This step will help you to stay organized, calm, and efficient.

As you practice, try to simulate the test environment as well as you can so that on test day all your techniques and strategies will feel natural. During your practice sessions, try to limit yourself to five sheets of paper (the number of noteboards you'll receive). While you can get more noteboards during the actual exam, you must turn over your current booklet of noteboards to the proctor before he or she leaves the testing room to get more. The clock doesn't stop while that happens. So, just practice with the equivalent of one set of noteboards for all your POE and calculations.

The Integrated Reasoning Section

In 2012, the GMAT gained a new section called Integrated Reasoning. This chapter reviews the basics of the new section, including a rundown on all four new question types.

Meet The Integrated Reasoning Section

The Integrated Reasoning section is 30 minutes long. You'll see it as the second section of your test. Officially, there are only 12 questions, which sounds pretty great. However, most of those questions have multiple parts. So, for example, a Table Analysis question—one of the new question types we'll discuss—usually has three statements that you need to evaluate. So, your answer to the question really consists of three separate responses. For the entire section, you'll actually need to select approximately 28 different responses.

Integrated Reasoning Is Not Adaptive

Unlike the Quantitative and Verbal sections, the Integrated Reasoning section is not adaptive. So, you won't see harder questions if you keep answering questions correctly. That's good news because it means that you'll more easily be able to focus your attention on the current question rather than worrying whether you got the previous question right!

Test writers refer to non-adaptive sections as linear. Pacing for a linear section is different from the pacing that we reviewed for the adaptive Quantitative and Verbal sections.

For Integrated Reasoning, pacing is motivated by two general principles.

Pacing Guidelines

1. Work the easier parts of each question first. As you'll see, many Integrated Reasoning questions call for more than one response per question. Work the easier parts of each question first.

2. Don't get stubborn. With so many questions to answer in only 30 minutes, the Integrated Reasoning section can seem very fast paced. Spending too much time on one question means that you may not get to see all of the questions. Sometimes it's best to guess and move on.

Integrated Reasoning Scores

The Integrated Reasoning section is scored on a scale from 1 to 8 in one-point increments. While GMAC has not released too many details about the way in which they calculate the score for this section of the test, there are two key facts to keep in mind.

- **Scoring is all or nothing.** Most Integrated Reasoning questions include multiple parts. To get credit for the question, you must select the correct response for each part. For example, Table Analysis questions generally include three statements that you must evaluate. If you select the wrong response for even one of these statements, you get no credit for the entire question.
- **There are experimental questions.** GMAC has stated that the Integrated Reasoning section contains experimental questions that do not count toward your score. They have not, however, stated how many experimental questions there are in the section. It's likely that two or three of the twelve questions in the section are experimental. If you find a question particularly difficult or time-consuming, it is worthwhile to remember that the question could be experimental.

To score the section, GMAC first calculates a raw score. You get one point for each non-experimental question that you get completely correct. Then, your raw score is converted to the 1 to 8 Integrated Reasoning scaled score.

There's a Calculator

There's an onscreen calculator available for the Integrated Reasoning section. The calculator is not available, however, for the Quantitative section. For the Quantitative section, you still need to perform any necessary calculations by hand.

The calculator for the Integrated Reasoning section is relatively basic. There are buttons to perform the four standard operations: addition, subtraction, multiplication, and division. In addition, buttons to take a square root, find a percent, and take a reciprocal round out the available functions. There are also buttons to store and recall a value in the calculator's memory.

To use the calculator, you'll need to open it by clicking on the 'calculator' button in the upper left corner of your screen. The calculator will generally open in the middle of your screen but you can move it around so that you can see the text of the problem or the numbers on any charts or graphs that are part of the question. The calculator is available for all Integrated Reasoning questions. You can enter a number into the calculator either by clicking on the onscreen number buttons or by typing the number using the keyboard.

Here's what the calculator looks like:

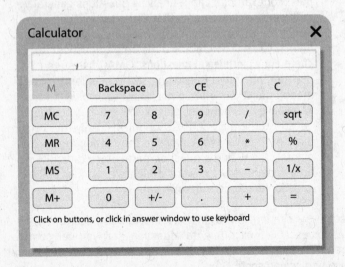

Crash Course for the GMAT

For the most part, the keys on the onscreen calculator work as you might expect. However, a few keys may not work as expected. Oddly enough, that's particularly true if you are used to using a more sophisticated calculator. So, here are few tips about using some of the calculator keys:

MC MC is the memory clear key. Use this key to wipe out any values that you have stored in the calculator's memory.

MR MR is the memory recall key. Use this key to return any value that you have stored in the memory to the calculation area. For example, if you want to divide the number currently on your screen by the number in the memory, you would enter the key sequence / MR =.

MS MS is the memory store key. Use this key to store the number currently on the screen in the calculator's memory.

M+ M+ is the memory addition key. Use this key to add the current onscreen number to the number in the calculator's memory. For example, if 2 is stored in the calculator's memory and 3 is on screen, then clicking M+ will result in 5 being stored in the calculator's memory.

Backspace Backspace is used to clear the last digit entered. Use this key to correct mistakes when entering numbers without clearing the entire number. For example, if you entered 23 but meant to enter 25, click backspace and then enter 5.

CE CE is the clear entry button. Use this button to correct a mistake when entering a longer calculation without starting over. For example, suppose you entered 2*3+5 but you meant to enter 2*3+9. If you click on CE right after you enter 5, your screen will show 6, the result of 2*3, and you can now enter +9= to finish your intended calculation.

| C |

C is the clear key. Use this key when you want to start a calculation over. In our previous example, if you click C after you enter 5, the intermediate result, 6, is not retained.

| sqrt |

sqrt is the square root key. Click this key after you enter the number for which you want to take the square root. For example, if you enter 4 sqrt, the result 2 will display on your screen.

| % |

% is the key used to take a percentage without entering a decimal. For example, if you want to take 20% of 400, enter 400*20%. The result 80 will now show on your screen. Note that you do not need to enter = after you click %.

| 1/x |

1/x is used to take a reciprocal. Click this key after you enter the number for which you want to take the reciprocal. For example, the keystrokes 2 followed by 1/x produces the result 0.5 on your screen. Again, note that you do not need to enter = after you click 1/x.

Be sure that you thoroughly understand the way the keys for the onscreen calculator work so as to avoid errors and wasted time when you take your GMAT.

The Question Types

There are four question types in the Integrated Reasoning section. While some of these questions test Critical Reasoning skills similar to those tested on the Verbal section, these question types are also used to test the same type of content that is tested in the Quantitative section. So, expect to calculate percents and averages. You'll also be asked to make a lot of inferences based on the data presented in the various charts, graphs, and tables that accompany the questions. So, the format of these questions may take some getting used to but the content will probably seem familiar.

Let's take a more detailed look at each of the new question types.

Crash Course for the GMAT

Table Analysis

Table Analysis questions present data in a table. If you've ever seen a spreadsheet—and really, who hasn't?—you'll feel right at home. Most tables have 5 to 10 columns and anywhere from 6 to 25 rows. You'll be able to sort the data in the table by each column heading. The sort function is fairly basic, however. If you're used to being able to sort first by a column such as state and then a column such as city to produce an alphabetical list of cities by state, you can't do that sort of sorting for these questions. You can sort only one column at a time.

Here's what a Table Analysis question looks like:

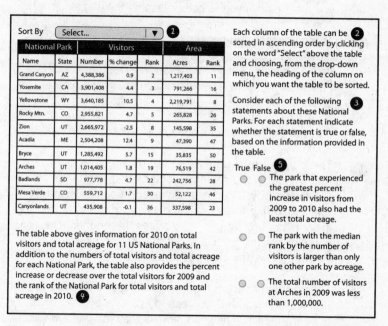

Sort By [Select... ▼] **1**

National Park		Visitors			Area	
Name	State	Number	% change	Rank	Acres	Rank
Grand Canyon	AZ	4,388,386	0.9	2	1,217,403	11
Yosemite	CA	3,901,408	4.4	3	791,266	16
Yellowstone	WY	3,640,185	10.5	4	2,219,791	8
Rocky Mtn.	CO	2,955,821	4.7	5	265,828	26
Zion	UT	2,665,972	-2.5	8	145,598	35
Acadia	ME	2,504,208	12.4	9	47,390	47
Bryce	UT	1,285,492	5.7	15	35,835	50
Arches	UT	1,014,405	1.8	19	76,519	42
Badlands	SD	977,778	4.7	22	242,756	28
Mesa Verde	CO	559,712	1.7	30	52,122	46
Canyonlands	UT	435,908	-0.1	36	337,598	23

The table above gives information for 2010 on total visitors and total acreage for 11 US National Parks. In addition to the numbers of total visitors and total acreage for each National Park, the table also provides the percent increase or decrease over the total visitors for 2009 and the rank of the National Park for total visitors and total acreage in 2010. **4**

Each column of the table can be **2** sorted in ascending order by clicking on the word "Select" above the table and choosing, from the drop-down menu, the heading of the column on which you want the table to be sorted.

Consider each of the following **3** statements about these National Parks. For each statement indicate whether the statement is true or false, based on the information provided in the table.

True False **5**

○ ○ The park that experienced the greatest percent increase in visitors from 2009 to 2010 also had the least total acreage.

○ ○ The park with the median rank by the number of visitors is larger than only one other park by acreage.

○ ○ The total number of visitors at Arches in 2009 was less than 1,000,000.

The circled numbers you see above will not appear on your screen when you take the Integrated Reasoning section. We've added those so we can talk about different parts of a Table Analysis question.

Here's what each circled number represents:

1 This is the Sort By drop-down box. When opened, you'll see all the different ways that you can sort the data in the table. In this table, for example, the possibilities are National Park Name, National Park State, Visitors Number, Visitors % change, Visitors Rank, Area Acreage, and Area Rank. You can always sort by every column.

2 These are the standard directions for a Table Analysis question. These directions are the same for every Table Analysis question. So, once you've read these directions, you don't really need to bother reading them again.

3 These lines are additional directions. These additional directions are slightly tailored to the question. However, they'll always tell you to base your answers on the information in the table. They always tell you which type of evaluation you are to make for each statement: true/false, yes/no, agree/disagree, and so on. Again, you can probably get by without reading these most of the time.

4 These lines explain the table. Mostly, this information will recap the column headings from the table. Occasionally, you can learn some additional information by reading this explanatory text. For example, the explanatory text for this table states that the Visitors Number column is for 2010 and that % change column shows the change from 2009 to 2010.

5 These statements are the questions. Typically, there are four statements and you need to evaluate and select an answer for each. The good news is that you can answer these in any order. However, if you try to move to the next question without selecting a response for one or more statements, a pop up window opens to inform you that you have not selected an answer for all statements. You cannot leave any part of the question blank.

If you've read through the statements, you may have noticed that the questions asked you to do things such as calculate a percentage or find a median. That's typical for Table Analysis questions. You've probably also realized just how helpful the sorting function can be in answering some questions.

Graphics Interpretation

Graphics Interpretation questions give you one chart, graph, or image and ask you to answer two questions based on that information. The questions are statements that include one drop-down box. You select your answer from the drop-down box to complete the statement.

Here's an example of a Graphics Interpretation question:

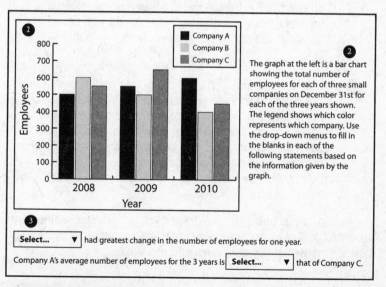

The graph at the left is a bar chart showing the total number of employees for each of three small companies on December 31st for each of the three years shown. The legend shows which color represents which company. Use the drop-down menus to fill in the blanks in each of the following statements based on the information given by the graph.

Select... ▼ had greatest change in the number of employees for one year.

Company A's average number of employees for the 3 years is Select... ▼ that of Company C.

As with the Table Analysis questions, we've added the circled numbers so we can point out the different things that you'll see on your screen for a Graphics Interpretation question. Here's what each circled number represents:

1 The chart, graph, or image is always in the upper left of the screen. As shown here, the chart will take up a good deal of the screen. It will certainly be large enough that you can clearly extract information from it. You can expect to see a variety of different types of charts or graphs including scatter plots, bar charts, line graphs, and circle (or pie) charts. For the most part, you'll see fairly standard types of graphs, however. Be sure to check out any labels on the axes as well as any sort of included legend.

2 These lines provide an explanation of the graph or chart. Mostly, you'll be told what the chart represents as well as what the individual lines, bars, or sectors may represent. Sometimes, you'll be given some additional information such as when measurements were made. For example, here you are told that the bars show the numbers of employees for each firm on December 31st of the year in question. This information is typically extraneous to answering the questions. The explanatory information always ends with the same line about selecting your answers from the drop-down menu.

3 These are the questions. Graphics Interpretation questions typically include two statements. You don't have to answer them in order, but you must answer both to move on to the next question. Each statement is typically a single sentence with one drop-down menu. Each drop-down menu typically includes three to five answer choices. Choose the answer choice that makes the statement true.

Graphics Analysis questions mostly ask you to find relationships and trends for the data. You can also be asked to calculate percentage increases or decreases, averages, and medians.

Two-Part Analysis

Next up is the Two-Part Analysis question. In many ways, the Two-Part Analysis question is most similar to a standard math question. You'll typically be presented with a word problem that essentially has two variables in it. You'll need to pick an answer for each variable that makes some condition in the problem true.

Here's an example of a Two-Part Analysis question:

Two families buy new refrigerators using installment plans. Family A makes an initial payment of $750. Family B makes an initial payment of $1,200. Both families make five additional payments to pay off the balance. Both families pay the same amount for their refrigerators, including all taxes, fees, and finance charges.

In the table below, identify a monthly payment, in dollars, for Family A and a monthly payment, in dollars, for Family B that are consistent with the installment plan described above. Make only one selection in each column. ②

Family A	Family B	Monthly payment (in dollars)
○	○	50
○	○	80
○	○	120 ③
○	○	160
○	○	250
○	○	300

As you might have surmised, we have once again added the circled numbers so we can described the different parts of the question. Here's what each circled number represents:

①   This first block of text is the actual problem. Here, you'll find the description of the two variables in the problem. You'll also find the condition that needs to be made true. As with any word problem, make sure that you read the information carefully. For these problems, you'll also want to make sure that you are clear about which information goes with the first variable and which information goes with the second.

2 This part of the problem tells you how to pick your answers. Mostly this part tells you to pick a value for column A and a value for column B based on the conditions of the problem. This part is mostly boiler-plate text that varies slightly from problem to problem.

3 These are the answer choices. Two-Part Analysis questions generally have five or six answer choices. You choose only one answer choice for each column. It is possible that the same number is the answer for both columns. So, if that's what your calculations indicate, go ahead and choose the same number for both columns.

Most Two-Part Analysis questions can be solved using math that is no more sophisticated than simple arithmetic. There is one exception to that, however. While most Two-Part Analysis questions are math problems, you may see one that looks like a Critical Reasoning question. For these, you'll be give an argument and you'll need to do something like pick one answer that strengthens and one answer that weakens the argument. For these questions, just use the methods from our Step 3: Arguments chapter.

Multi-Source Reasoning

Finally, we come to the Multi-Source Reasoning question. Multi-Source Reasoning questions present information on tabs. The information can be text, charts, graphs, or a combination. In other words, GMAC can put almost anything on the tabs! The layout looks a little bit like Reading Comprehension because the tabbed information is on the left side of your screen while the right side shows the questions.

Here's an example of a Multi-Source Reasoning question:

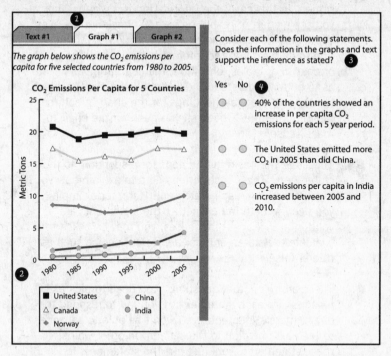

Again, we've added circled numbers to indicate the different parts of the question. Here's what each circled number represents:

1 The tabs appear across the top left of the screen. Some questions have two tabs and some, as in this example, have three. The tabs typically give you some sort of indication about what's on the tab. The currently selected tab is white while the unselected tabs are grey. GMAC can put almost anything on each tab including graphs, tables, charts, text, or some combination. It's a good idea to take a few seconds to get your bearings before attempting the questions. Make sure you know what is on each tab and how the information on one tab relates to information on the other tab or tabs.

2 The information for each tab appears on the left of the screen. In this case, the information is a graph. When you see a chart or graph, be sure to check out the axes. You'll also want to look for a legend or other information to help explain the information shown by the graph or chart. For tables, check out the column headings so as to better understand the table. Finally, don't neglect to read any supplied headings for the chart, graph, or table. Sometimes, that's all you need for the chart to make sense.

3 These are the basic instructions for responding to the statements. These instructions help to explain how you need to evaluate each statement. Here, for example, you need to determine whether the statements are valid inferences. In other cases, you may be asked to evaluate the statements for a different choice such as true or false.

4 These are the actual questions. You need to pick a response for each statement. If you fail to respond to one or more statements, you won't be able to advance to the next question in the section. In other words, these statements work just like the statements for the Table Analysis question type.

Multi-Source Reasoning questions usually come in sets. Each set typically consists of three separate questions. Two of those questions are typically in the statement style as shown in the example above. It's also possible to get a standard multiple-choice question as part of the set. For a standard multiple choice question, there are five answer choices and you select one response.

You may need information from more than one tab to respond to a statement or multiple-choice question. Don't forget to think about the information on the other tabs while evaluating the statements. That's why it's important to take a few moments to get familiar with what's on each tab before starting work on the questions.

PART II

Ten Steps to the GMAT

Sentence Correction

Sentence correction questions comprise about one-third, or 14, of the questions on your GMAT Verbal section. According to GMAC, these questions are "designed to measure your correct use of grammar, your ability to form clear and effective sentences and your capacity to choose the most appropriate words."

Doing well on this section has little to do with your ability to speak English fluently. Written English (with very strict rules of grammar) is what the GMAT is all about. See whether you can spot the grammatical flaw in the following sentence:

> Every day trader uses publications like *The Wall Street Journal* and *The Financial Times* to make their decisions.

Don't see anything wrong with the sentence? That's what GMAC is hoping. Although it sounds perfectly normal when spoken out loud, the sentence actually contains a grammatical error (for the record, the error is that the word their should be replaced with his or her for pronoun agreement).

On the GMAT, sentence correction questions consist of a sentence, part of which is underlined, followed by five answer choices that represent different ways of writing the underlined portion of the sentence. A single word, a short phrase, or the entire sentence may be underlined. The first answer choice, (A), always repeats the underlined portion of the original sentence with no changes. Answer choices (B), (C), (D), and (E) provide alternate ways of expressing the same idea.

Most people approach sentence correction questions in the wrong way. The average test taker, for example, reads the sentence, spots what he or she thinks is the error in the underlined portion, mentally fixes the sentence, and chooses the answer choice that comes closest to what sounds right to him or her. There are a couple of problems with this approach. One, GMAC deliberately makes the errors hard to spot, and two, GMAC is very good at writing incorrect answer choices.

Some incorrect answer choices repeat a grammatical error in the original sentence, rewriting another part of the sentence that didn't originally contain an error. Others fix the error of the original sentence but introduce a new error. To avoid falling into the traps GMAC sets for you on sentence correction, follow our approach.

The Three-Step Approach

The key to cracking sentence correction questions is to know what types of grammatical errors GMAC likes to test most. This, along with a systematic use of Process of Elimination, will help you do well on this section. The Three-Step Approach you'll use is listed below.

Let's take a look at a sentence correction question and try out the Three-Step Approach:

> While preparing his bid, <u>the contractor estimated the cost of the building materials at $50,000</u>.
>
> ○   the contractor estimated the cost of the building materials at $50,000
>
> ○   the contractor estimated at $50,000 the cost of the building materials
>
> ○   the contractor estimated the cost of the building materials to be $50,000
>
> ○   the cost of the building materials was estimated by the contractor at $50,000
>
> ○   the cost of the building materials was estimated by the contractor to be $50,000

Step 1: Read the Question and Identify the Error. Read the entire sentence closely, making sure you understand the context of the underlined portion. Let's assume you spot the error right away: the incorrect idiom *estimated...at*.

Step 2: Eliminate All Answer Choices Containing That Error. Since you have spotted the error, you can go through the answer choices (write A, B, C, D, E on your noteboard) and eliminate all choices that repeat the incorrect idiom. That gets rid of answer choices (A), (B), and (D).

Step 3: Look for Grammar Errors in the Remaining Answer Choices and Eliminate Them. Compare answer choices (C) and (E). If you recognize the fact that the phrase While *preparing his bid* must modify the noun *contractor*, then you know that (E) is incorrect. Eliminate it, and you're left with (C), which is the correct answer.

Plan B

Perhaps you don't remember the difference between *that* and *which*. Don't worry—we'll review this, along with several other common constructions and idioms, later in this chapter. But let's imagine for a moment that, even after poring over all the material in this chapter, you see a sentence correction question and cannot identify the error. There are two possible reasons for this. The error may be very difficult to identify, or the sentence may not contain an error at all.

Don't Overcorrect

Remember that the sentence may be correct as it is written. Answer choice (A) always repeats the underlined portion of the sentence exactly as it appears in the original sentence, and it *will* be correct some of the time. If you've gone through Step 1 and cannot spot the error, go straight to the answer choices. You may find that you're left with the original sentence.

Be careful, too, of what sounds good. The GMAT tests the strict rules of written grammar, so relying on your ear to lead you to the correct answer is not a good strategy.

More on Process of Elimination

Take another look at the answer choices for the sentence about the contractor. Notice that two of the answer choices begin with *the cost* and three begin with the *contractor*. We call this a 2/3 split, and this pattern—or focus on *contractor v. cost*—can clue you in to the grammar error that the sentence is testing. In this case, if you can determine whether the *contractor* or the *cost* is incorrect, you can eliminate that entire set of answer choices.

Six Commonly Tested Errors

You now have an overview of sentence correction problems and the basic techniques for approaching them. Now we'll list six commonly tested errors and teach you how to spot and fix each one.

Misplaced Modifier

Rule: A descriptive word or phrase should be placed immediately before or after the thing that it modifies.

How to spot it: Two phrases are separated by a comma and one or both of them are underlined.

How to fix it: Choose an answer choice that puts the modifying phrase and the object it's modifying right next to each other (separated by a comma).

Example:

> A dairy cow known for its gentle temperament, the milk of the Jersey is high in fat content and suitable for either drinking or processing.
>
> ∅ the milk of the Jersey is high in fat content and suitable for either drinking or processing
>
> ∅ the milk of the Jersey is high in fat content, suited for either drinking or processing
>
> ○ the Jersey gives milk that is high in fat content and suitable for either drinking or processing
>
> ∅ the milk of the Jersey is high in fat content and suitable either to drink or to process
>
> ∅ the Jersey gives milk that is high in fat content, suitable for either drinking or processing

Step 1: **Read the Question and Identify the Error.** Since the underlined portion of the sentence comes directly after a comma, there is a good chance that the error here is a misplaced modifier. What does the modifying phrase, *A dairy cow known for its gentle temperament*, modify— the cow or the milk? It should modify the cow, but as the sentence is written, the modifying phrase modifies the milk.

Step 2: **Eliminate All Answer Choices Containing That Error.** Since you've identified the error, you can now eliminate all the answer choices in the 2/3 split that contain the same error—(A), (B), and (D)—and you're down to two answer choices.

Step 3: **Look for Grammar Errors in the Remaining Answer Choices and Eliminate Them.** Compare answer choices (C) and (E)—what's the difference between them? Choice (C) contains the word *and*, while choice (E) simply has a comma. Which is right? Well, answer choice (E), in which the *and* is replaced with a comma, contains the modifying phrase *suitable for either drinking or processing*. This phrase incorrectly modifies *fat content*, which precedes it. Answer choice (E) is grammatically incorrect, so eliminate it. Choice (C) is the correct answer.

Pronouns

Rule: A pronoun must clearly refer to a noun, and must agree with that noun in gender and number.

How to spot it: A pronoun is in the underlined portion of the sentence.

How to fix it: Identify the pronoun and the noun it replaces. Change the pronoun so that it agrees with the noun.

Example:

> The average Olympic athlete begins training at
> the age of 10, although <u>they may not compete</u>
> for several more years.
>
> ○ they may not compete
> ○ they might not compete
> ○ she may not compete
> ○ it does not compete
> ○ competition is not their goal

Step 1: Read the Sentence and Identify the Error. The error must
be in either the pronoun or verb use, since that's
pretty much all the underlined portion of the sentence
contains. The way to determine whether *they* is the
correct pronoun is to try to match it with the noun it
replaces, in this case, *athlete*. *Athlete* is singular, so
you need a singular pronoun (not a plural one, like
they) such as *he* or *she* (it cannot refer to people).

If you do not immediately know that the pronoun is incorrect, you
can look through the answer choices and start eliminating those
that definitely contain an error. But when you see a pronoun in the
underlined portion of the sentence, you should always check it—
pronoun errors are very common on the GMAT.

Step 2: Eliminate All Answer Choices Containing That Error. The
error is that the sentence contains a singular noun and
a plural pronoun. Eliminate answer choices (A), (B),
and (E) because all the pronouns in these choices are
plural.

**Step 3: Look for Grammar Errors in the Remaining Answer Choices
and Eliminate Them.** Compare answer choices (C) and
(D). You know that it cannot refer to people, so eliminate choice (D). Answer choice (C) is the answer.

Subject/Verb Agreement

Rule: A verb must agree in number with its subject.

How to spot it: Typically, in a sentence with a subject/verb error, GMAC places the subject and verb as far away from each other as possible.

How to fix it: Identify the subject and verb of the sentence or phrase, and make sure they agree in number.

Example:

> The members of the newest wave of world-class chefs have created a cuisine characterized not only by excellence but also eclecticism: the traditional techniques of French cuisine form a foundation <u>to which is added Latin American, Asian, and African elements</u>.

- ⌀ to which is added Latin American, Asian, and African elements
- ⌀ added to which is Latin American, Asian, and African elements
- ◯ to which Latin American, Asian, and African elements are added
- ⌀ with Latin American, Asian, and African elements being added to it
- ⌀ and, in addition, Latin American, Asian, and African elements are added

Step 1: Read the Sentence and Identify the Error. Since there is a verb in the underlined portion, you should suspect subject/verb agreement as the possible source of error. As you can see, the verb *is added* is singular and doesn't agree with the noun it is paired with, in this case, *elements* which is plural. So what you need is the plural verb *are added*.

Step 2: Eliminate All Answer Choices Containing That Error. Eliminating the singular verbs gets rid of choices (A) and (B).

Step 3: **Look for Grammar Errors in the Remaining Answer Choices and Eliminate Them.** Nothing appears to be wrong with answer choice (C). It has the plural verb *are added* and although it's a modifying phrase, it modifies the word immediately before it, *foundation*. Choice (D), on the other hand, contains the word *being*, which is not an acceptable way to conjugate a verb (the *ing* ending goes on the main verb, not the helping verb). Therefore, choice (D) is incorrect. Keep your eye out for the word *being*; GMAC loves to use it, but it is almost always used incorrectly. Answer choice (E) is redundant, *and... in addition...added*, and should be eliminated. Choice (C) is the best answer.

Another note on subject/verb agreement: *No one* is singular, and *every* modifies a singular noun; both indicate that the verb that follows should be singular. The word *none* is trickier; it can be singular or plural depending on the context.

Examples:

> No one who lives here is at home.

> None of the executives hired last year is still employed here.

> Every burglary in the neighborhood is the work of a well-known jewel thief.

Parallel Construction

Rule: Words, phrases, and clauses that are either in a list or being compared must all contain the same parts of speech and must *look* the same.

How to spot it: If the sentence contains a list or comparison, you should probably look for a parallel construction error.

How to fix it: Find the list or comparison in the nonunderlined portion of the sentence. Change the nonmatching member of the list or comparison so that it matches the other members.

Example:

> General contracting firms are investigating changes in construction techniques that would permit contractors to reduce the time required to complete construction of a building, <u>decrease the amount of raw material needed during construction, and to avoid changes that require contractors that revise blueprints</u> and redraft working plans.

 decrease the amount of raw material needed during construction, and to avoid changes that require contractors that revise blueprints

 decrease the amount of raw material needed during construction, and avoiding changes that require contractors revising blueprints

 to decrease the amount of raw material needed during construction, and avoiding changes that require contractors to revise blueprints

 to decrease the amount raw material needed during construction, avoiding changes that require contractors that revise blueprints

 to decrease the amount of raw material needed during construction, and to avoid changes that require contractors to revise blueprints

Step 1: **Read the Sentence and Identify the Error.** You have both *decrease* and *to avoid* in the underlined portion. These words are not parallel. Furthermore, the verb *require* must be followed by an infinitive, in this case, *to revise*.

Step 2: **Eliminate All Answer Choices Containing That Error.** Your list starts with *to reduce* in the nonunderlined portion. When you have a list of infinitives like this one, the initial *to* can cover all the verbs listed. So a good answer choice would read *decrease...and avoid* or to decrease...and to avoid. Get rid of choice (A), *decrease...and to avoid*; choice (B), *decrease...and avoiding*; and choice (C), *to decrease...and avoiding*, because none of these is parallel.

Step 3: Look for Grammar Errors in the Remaining Answer Choices and Eliminate Them. Answer choice (D) reads to *decrease..., avoiding* making the final phrase a modifier. *Avoiding changes* does not modify construction, so eliminate it. Choice (E) reads *to decrease...and to avoid*, which is an acceptable way to complete this list.

That's an example of a parallel construction containing a list. Let's look at one that contains a comparison.

Example:

The rules of rugby are more liberal <u>than soccer</u>.

- ⊗ than soccer
- ⊗ as soccer
- ⊗ as those of soccer
- ◯ than those of soccer
- ⊗ than soccer is

Step 1: Read the Sentence and Identify the Error. The word *than* is underlined, so you're dealing with a parallel construction that centers on a comparison. Identify what you're comparing (the rules of rugby and the rules of soccer) and look for an answer choice that makes the comparison clear. The error here is that the way the sentence currently reads, you're comparing *rules* to *soccer*.

Step 2: Eliminate All Answer Choices Containing That Error. Eliminate answer choices (A), (B), and (E), because they all compare *rules* to *soccer*.

Step 3: Look for Grammar Errors in the Remaining Answer Choices and Eliminate Them. Choices (C) and (D) differ only in that choice (C) contains as and choice (D) contains *than*. The correct idiom is *more...than*. Choice (D) is the best answer.

Verb Tense

Simple past, present perfect, and past perfect are the three verb tenses most commonly tested on the GMAT. You do not need to worry about what they're called; focus on learning how to identify their correct usage.

Rule:

Use the	When an action started in the past and...	
Simple Past	Has ceased to occur	Alex looked puzzled when you told him the news.
Present Perfect	Continues to the present	As long as I have known him, Alex has looked puzzled in meetings.
Past Perfect	Was completed before some other past action began.	Alex had always looked puzzled in meetings until he got a new boss.

How to spot it: The sentence contains an action, or it contains a series of actions occurring at different times.

How to fix it: Identify the sequence of events in the sentence. Use the table above to determine the correct verb tense.

Example:

Some epidemiologists believe that the Ebola virus <u>has originated from an animal host in a less populated region of Africa and has flourished in areas</u> where there is more frequent contact between humans and wild animals.

- ~~has originated from an animal host in a less populated region of Africa and has flourished in areas~~
- ○ originated from an animal host in a less populated region of Africa and has flourished in areas
- ~~has originated from an animal host in a less populated region of Africa and had flourished in areas~~
- ~~originated from an animal host in a less populated region of Africa and had flourished in areas~~
- ~~originated from an animal host in a less populated region of Africa and flourished in areas~~

Step 1: **Read the Sentence and Identify the Error.** The series of events (*has originated...has flourished*) in the under-lined portion points to a verb tense error. The first event is one that can occur only once (something can *originate* only once) and thus calls for the simple past, *originated*. The second event began in the past and continues into the present, so *has flourished* is correct.

Step 2: **Eliminate All Answer Choices Containing That Error.** The 2/3 split with *originated/has originated* allows you to eliminate choices (A) and (C).

Step 3: **Look for Grammar Errors in the Remaining Answer Choices and Eliminate Them.** Of the remaining answer choices, only choice (B) contains the correct tense *has flourished*.

Idioms and Style

The last category of grammar errors GMAC likes to test is actually a list of grammatical constructions called idioms. There is no strict rule governing the use of idioms; there is simply a list of words and phrases you'll need to memorize. The good news is that once you learn to recognize them, you'll always know how to fix them. A list of the 50 most common idiomatic phrases and constructions is located at the end of this chapter.

Let's wrap up this chapter with some pointers on style. Occasionally, you'll be left with two answer choices that differ only in style. In this case, eliminate the answer choice that is redundant, wordier, or written in the passive voice.

Example:

> After Al Gore spent weeks trying to resuscitate his dying campaign, <u>yielding the nomination to Bill Bradley was chosen by Gore</u> rather than to face further humiliation and bankruptcy.
>
> ○   yielding the nomination to Bill Bradley was chosen by Gore
>
> ○   to yield the nomination to Bill Bradley was chosen by Gore
>
> ○   Gore chose to yield the nomination to Bill Bradley
>
> ○   Gore chose yielding the nomination to Bill Bradley
>
> ○   yielding the nomination to Bill Bradley

Step 1:   **Read the Sentence and Identify the Error.** Did you see that the error was one of parallel construction; *yielding ...rather than face? Good.*

Step 2:   **Eliminate All Answer Choices Containing That Error.** This gets rid of choices (A), (D), and (E).

Step 3:   **Look for Grammar Errors in the Remaining Answer Choices and Eliminate Them.** Answer choices (B) and (C) say the same thing, and both are grammatically correct, but choice (B) is written in the passive voice. So although there is nothing technically wrong with (B), it is very awkward and confusing to read. Choice (C) is a better answer.

Idioms

Here are fifty of the most frequently tested idiomatic constructions on the GMAT:

1. Where *or* when vs. that *or* in which

Do not use *where* or *when* instead of *in which* or *that*. These words are most commonly misused in this way:

Incorrect:

The talk show host agitated the guests to the point *where* they were throwing chairs at each other.

A mall is *where* people can shop at many stores under one roof.

Correct:

The talk show host agitated the guests to the point *that* they were throwing chairs at each other.

A mall is a group of stores under one roof.

Use *where* only when you're referring to an actual location.

That desk is *where* I spend countless hours working at my thankless job.

Use *when* only to denote a moment in time.

I'll go out with you *when* the clock strikes thirteen, and not a moment sooner.

2. Who vs. whom

Use *who* when you need a subject pronoun and whom when you need an object pronoun.

Who left the door open?

I can't wait to see *whom* she'll bring to dinner this time.

If you tend to confuse these two, try replacing *who* or *whom* with *he* or *him*. If the sentence or clause calls for *he*, use *who*; if it calls for *him*, use *whom*.

He left the door open. (Use *who*.)

...she'll bring him to dinner this time. (Use *whom*.)

3. Not only...but also

You are *not only* clever *but also* charming.

4. Not so...as

I am *not so* foolish as to fall for that a third time.

5. Not...but

The basketball player is *not* tall, *but* he is fast.

6. Either...or

I'll take *either* a BMW *or* a Lexus; I'm not particular.

7. Neither...nor

I will eat *neither* tomatoes *nor* Brussels sprouts; they smell funny.

8. Both...and

You should admit you're afraid of *both* clowns *and* elephants.

9. More...than

That weightlifter has *more* muscle in his head *than* he has brains.

10. Comparatives

Two separate sets of words are used when making comparisons. Use the first set when you are comparing only two things. Use the second set when you are comparing three or more things.

Only two things	Three or more things
More	Most
–er	–est
Between	Among

Only two things:

Between cake and ice cream, I like ice cream *more*.

Three or more things:

Among the three sisters, Cinderella was the *most* beautiful.

11. The more...the –er

The *more* you eat, the fatter you get.

12. Just as...so too

Just as I have found my cell phone indispensable, *so* you will *too*.

13. As...as

Washing my car in the winter is not *as* easy *as* it is in the summer.

14. Quantity words

Quantity words are tested on the GMAT because they are commonly confused. If you can physically count the things you're referring to, use the words in the first column. If you can't, use the words in the second column.

Can be counted	Cannot be counted
Many	Much
Number	Amount
Fewer	Less

Can be counted:

Give a child as *many* hugs as you can.

No human can read that *number* of pages in an hour.

She worked *fewer* hours than I did.

Cannot be counted:

Give a child as *much* love as you can.

No human can read that *amount* of material in an hour.

She worked *less* time than I did.

15. The number of vs. A number of

When you use *the number of*, you should use a singular verb (the number is singular).

The number of excuses grows every time he tells the story.

But when you use *a number of*, use a plural verb, as *a number of* something is a multitude.

A number of survivors of the plane crash *are* holding a press conference.

16. The same...as

Although she looks much older, my chemistry teacher is *the same* age *as* my mother.

17. Different from

You are no *different from* me; we both want success.

18. Superior...to

American Idol is a *superior* television show *to Survivor*.

19. Distinguish...from

Dazed by the battle, the soldier could no longer *distinguish* friend *from* foe.

20. Associate with

My dad says I can no longer *associate with* you.

21. Between...and

April found herself choosing *between* the devil *and* the deep blue sea.

22. Contrast...with

If you *contrast* one politician's ethics *with* another's, you will find no difference.

23. Responsibility to

It is my *responsibility to* feed the parakeet.

24. Responsible for

I am *responsible for* feeding the parakeet.

25. Require . . . to

Sheep herding *requires* a shepherd *to* stay with his flock at all times.

26. Forbid...to

I *forbid* you *to* interrupt me again.

27. Prohibit...from

I can physically *prohibit* you *from* interrupting me again.

28. Worry about

She *worried about* finding a place to hide the loot.

29. Permit to

Convicted felons are not *permitted to* vote.

30. Try to

Please *try to* chew with your mouth closed at the awards dinner tonight.

31. Ability...to

He has an *ability to* turn around a failing business.

32. Believe...to be

I no longer *believe* the tooth fairy *to be* real.

33. Consider

Many *consider* Henry Kissinger the greatest statesman of the twentieth century.

34. Estimate...to be

The sideshow barker *estimated* Henry *to be* a fool.

35. Define...as

Some Republicans *define* welfare abuse *as* the primary evil in America.

36. Regard...as

Shakespeare is *regarded as* the greatest playwright of all time.

37. Think of...as

She *thinks of* me *as* just a friend.

38. See...as

My father *sees* a large investment portfolio *as* a sign of success.

39. Native

Native requires two different constructions: one when it's a noun, and a different one when it's used as an adjective.

Noun: *Native...of*

Not surprisingly, Donald Trump is a *native of* New York City.

Adjective: *Native...to*

Okra is *native to* Africa.

40. That vs. which

Misusing the words *that* and *which* is a very common mistake in English. Both *that* and *which* are used to introduce modifiers. The key is to determine whether the modifying information is required or whether it's extraneous. If the information is required, use that.

That:

The lawnmower *that* you came to fix is in the garage.

You need the information *that you came to fix* so you know which lawnmower the speaker is talking about.

Which:

The lawnmower, *which* is in the garage, is broken beyond repair.

The sentence is about the lawnmower and its state of disrepair. The information about where it is located (*which is in the garage*) is extraneous.

41. As vs. like

A good rule of thumb for the word *like* is to avoid it if another word or phrase will work. *As* is used to compare noun/verb combinations. *Like* is used when comparing only nouns.

He does not bathe every day, *as* I do.

That car is just *like* one my father had.

42. Like vs. such as

Again, don't use *like* if another word or phrase will do. Use *such as* when you mean "*for example*," and use *like* when you mean "*similar to*."

> Many of the top designers, *such as* Ralph Lauren and Donna Karan, have less expensive lines as well.

> Why must you act *like* a four-year-old?

43. From...to

> Route 66 is a highway that runs *from* Chicago *to* Los Angeles.

44. Attribute...to

> Many theories in contemporary psychology are *attributed to* Freud.

45. Credit...with

> Benjamin Franklin is *credited with* the invention of the U.S. postal system.

46. Each vs. all or both

Use *each* when you want to emphasize that items are separate. Use *both* or *all* when you want to emphasize that items are together or similar.

> *Each* of the schools he applied to has its own strengths.

> *Both* of the programs were highly regarded.

> *All* of the schools offer financial assistance.

47. So...that

> She was *so* blunt *that* many considered her rude.

48. So...as to be

> Joe is *so* smart *as to be* intimidating.

49. Hypothesis that

> A *hypothesis that* the aluminum in soda cans causes Alzheimer's disease is circulating on the Internet.

50. Target...at

> Many cigarette companies *target* their advertising *at* children.

Math
Definitions

Welcome back to ninth grade! The math on the GMAT, while some-times presented in a potentially confusing way, does not rely on your ability to perform any advanced mathematical operations. Once you understand what each problem is asking, you will be doing rela-tively simple, straightforward calculations, such as multiplying, converting fractions to decimals, factoring, and solving for x.

Mathematical Definitions and the Basics

We know it's probably been a while since you did ninth-grade math, so let's start off with a review of some of the vocabulary and math-ematical operations you'll encounter on the GMAT.

Coefficient

In the expression $3xy$, the number 3 is called the **coefficient**.

Consecutive

Consecutive describes integers listed in ascending order, which are separated by the same interval. The numbers 1, 2, 3, 4 are consecu-tive integers, and the numbers 2, 4, 6, 8 are consecutive even integers.

Decimals

Like fractions, **decimals** are a way of expressing parts of a whole. When given the option of working with fractions or decimals, fractions tend to be simpler and safer, but you'll also need to be comfortable adding, subtracting, multiplying, and dividing decimal expressions.

Adding/Subtracting Decimals

Most of us add decimals all the time and don't even realize it. Every time you figure out a tip in a restaurant, for instance, and pay your bill, you're adding decimals. To add or subtract decimals, just line up the decimal points, and add or subtract as you normally would.

Crash Course for the GMAT

Examples:

$$\begin{array}{r} 50.650 \\ +\ 28.123 \\ \hline 78.773 \end{array} \qquad \begin{array}{r} 35.958 \\ -\ 13.012 \\ \hline 22.946 \end{array}$$

Multiplying Decimals

To multiply decimals, start by ignoring the decimals and multiply the numbers as you normally would. Then add the total number of decimal places to the right of the decimal point in the numbers you multiplied, and put the decimal point the same number of digits over from the right, in your product.

Example:

$$\begin{array}{r} 5.2 \\ \times\ 2.5 \\ \hline 260 \\ 1040 \\ \hline 1300 \end{array}$$

There is one place to the right of each of the original multiples, so move the decimal point over two from the right, in the answer, to get 13.00.

Difference

The result of subtraction is called the **difference**.

Digit

The **digits** are 0, 1, 2, 3, 4, 5, 6, 7, 8, and 9—the numbers you see on a telephone. GMAT math problems might ask you to either count digits or supply a missing digit. Try counting the digits in 2654.189. There are seven.

Distinct

Distinct is simply a mathematical way of saying "different." So when you are asked to count the distinct prime factors of 12, you would answer that there are two—2 and 3. Even though $12 = 2 \times 2 \times 3$, you can count 2 only once.

Dividend

The number you are dividing another number *into* is the **dividend**. In the division $6 \div 2$, the number 6 is the dividend.

Divisible

When a number can be divided evenly by another number, it is said to be **divisible** by that number. So 6 is divisible by 3, but is not divisible by 4. The GMAT, however, is more likely to ask you whether 728 is divisible by 4. (Yes, it is.)

Some rules to help you check quickly for divisibility.

A number is divisible by	If
2	It ends in 0, 2, 4, 6, or 8.
3	The sum of its digits is divisible by 3.
4	The last two digits, considered as a number, are divisible by 4. Example: Take 728. The last two digits form the number 28, which is divisible by 4.
5	It ends in 5 or 0.
6	It is divisible by both 2 and 3.
7	There is no easy test for divisibility by 7, but you won't be asked about it, either.

| 8 | There is no easy test, but in a pinch, you can divide by 2 and check whether or not the resulting number is divisible by 4. |
| 9 | The sum of its digits is a multiple of 9. |

Even/Odd Numbers

An **even** number is one that can be divided evenly by 2. Even numbers are whole numbers that end in 2, 4, 6, 8, or 0. The number zero (0) is considered even.

An **odd** number is a whole number that, when divided by two, yields a remainder of 1. Odd numbers end in 1, 3, 5, 7, or 9.

Exponent

An **exponent** simply tells you to "multiply this number by itself x times." So $2^3 = 2 \times 2 \times 2$, or 8. The number you multiply is called the **base**, and the little superscript number, which tells you the number of times to multiply the base, is called an exponent, or a **power**. So in 3^2, 3 is the base and 2 is the power, or **exponent**.

Here are some more rules about exponents:

Any number to the power of 1 is itself: $5^1 = 5$

Any number to the power of 0 is 1: $5^0 = 1$

Any positive number greater than 1, raised to a power greater than 1 becomes larger. For example, $3^2 = 9$.

Any negative number raised to an even power becomes positive, but any negative number raised to an odd power stays negative. So $(-3)^4 = 81$, but $(-3)^3 = -27$.

Any fraction between 0 and 1 that's raised to a power greater than 1 becomes smaller. For example, $\left(\frac{1}{2}\right)^2 = \frac{1}{4}$.

Negative exponents—when you see a negative exponent, just turn the base into a fraction by putting a 1 over it and proceed as you would with a nonnegative exponent. So $3^{-2} = \left(\dfrac{1}{3}\right)^2 = \dfrac{1}{9}$.

Fractional Exponents

Fractional exponents are another form of writing roots. For example, $2^{\frac{1}{3}} = \sqrt[3]{2}$. See *Square Root* for more information.

Adding and Subtracting Exponents

To add and subtract exponents, both the base and the power must be the same. If they are, just add or subtract the coefficients. So $3x^2 + 5x^2 = 8x^2$ and $5x^2 - 3x^2 = 2x^2$.

Multiplying and Dividing Exponents

When multiplying or dividing exponents, make sure that the bases are the same. To multiply, add the exponents and multiply the coefficients. To divide, subtract the exponents and divide the coefficients.

Examples:

$$3x^2 \times 5x^3 = 15x^5 \text{ and } \frac{15x^6}{3x^2} = 5x^4$$

Factors

Factors are numbers that can be divided into another number without leaving a remainder. For example, the numbers 1, 2, 3, 4, 6, and 12 are the factors of 12.

Fractions

A fraction is the most basic expression of part or parts of a whole.

For example, if a whole pizza has 8 slices and James eats 3, he has eaten $\frac{3}{8}$ of the pizza.

Numerator/Denominator

The top number in a fraction is called the **numerator**, and the bottom number is called the **denominator**.

Reducing Fractions

On the GMAT, fractions should be expressed in their most reduced form. Therefore, you should simplify your answers, for instance, by reducing fractions. To reduce a fraction, simply find a number that's a factor of both its numerator and denominator, and factor it out, like this:

$$\frac{35}{49} = \frac{5 \times 7}{7 \times 7} = \frac{5}{7} \times \frac{7}{7} = \frac{5}{7} \times 1 = \frac{5}{7}$$

Reducing a fraction makes it easier to work with, which makes it less likely that you'll commit an error. Common factors to start with when you're reducing are 2, 3, and 5.

Adding/Subtracting Fractions

To add or subtract two fractions that have the same denominator, simply add or subtract their numerators, like this:

$$\frac{3}{4} + \frac{1}{4} = \frac{4}{4}, \text{ or } 1$$

If the numbers in the denominators are different, the process of adding or subtracting involves a couple of extra steps. The **Bowtie** is a simple method to use when you must add or subtract fractions with different denominators.

Here's an example:

$$\frac{5}{8} + \frac{3}{5}$$

To use the Bowtie method, first multiply straight across the bottom of the fraction to find a common denominator. Then multiply top to bottom, top to bottom, like a bowtie. Finally, add or subtract to find the numerator.

$$\frac{5}{8} + \frac{3}{5} = \overset{25}{\underset{}{\frac{5}{8}}} \bowtie \overset{24}{\underset{}{\frac{3}{5}}} = \frac{25 + 24}{8 \times 5} = \frac{49}{40}$$

Multiplying and Dividing Fractions

When multiplying two or more fractions, just multiply their numerators and then their denominators.

$$\frac{2}{5} \times \frac{3}{4} = \frac{2 \times 3}{5 \times 4} = \frac{6}{20} = \frac{3}{10}$$

Dividing fractions works a lot like multiplying fractions, with one important extra step. To divide fractions, multiply the first by the **reciprocal** of the second. (The term *reciprocal* is defined later in this list.) So flip the second fraction and multiply in the regular way.

$$\frac{2}{5} \div \frac{3}{4} = \frac{2}{5} \times \frac{4}{3} = \frac{2 \times 4}{5 \times 3} = \frac{8}{15}$$

Cross-Multiplication

To solve an equation that contains two *equal* fractions containing variables, you can simply **cross-multiply**, or multiply the numerator of each fraction by the denominator of the other.

Here's an example:

$$\frac{3x}{4} = \frac{3}{2}$$

Cross-multiply the numerator of the first fraction by the denominator of the second, and vice versa.

$$\frac{3x}{4} = \frac{3}{2}$$

$$(3x)(2) = (3)(4)$$

$$6x = 12$$

$$x = 2$$

Integer

An **integer** is any whole number, either positive or negative. Zero is considered to be an integer. So –3, 100, and 0 are integers.

Multiple

The result of multiplying any number by any other number is called a **multiple**. The numbers 8, 16, and 424 are all multiples of 4.

Order of Operations

Order of operations refers to just what it sounds like: the order in which mathematical operations are to be performed. There's a phrase that will help you remember all the operations in their proper order: **P**lease **E**xcuse **M**y **D**ear **A**unt **S**ally. It stands for **P**arentheses, **E**xponents, **M**ultiplication, **D**ivision, **A**ddition, and **S**ubtraction. Start with the parentheses and work your way from inside to outside. Next come exponents. Then, perform multiplication and division, from left to right. Last, perform any remaining addition and subtraction, again from left to right.

Consider this example:

$$2 + 10 \times 6$$

If you follow the order of operations and work multiplication before addition, you get

$$2 + (10 \times 6)$$

$$2 + (60)$$

You'll arrive at the correct answer, 62.

If you simply worked from left to right, you'd get

$$(2 + 10) \times 6$$

$$12 \times 6$$

which is equal to 72; that's incorrect.

Positive/Negative Numbers

A **positive number** is any number greater than 0. So $\frac{1}{4}$ is a positive number, as is 5,000, but 0 is not.

Any number that's less than 0 is a **negative number**. The number −15 is negative. Zero is not.

Prime Numbers

Prime numbers have exactly two distinct factors: 1 and themselves. For example, 13 is a prime number because its only factors are 1 and 13. The number 1 is not prime.

Product

The result of multiplication is called the **product**.

Quotient

The result of division is called the **quotient**.

Reciprocal

The inverse of a number or fraction is a **reciprocal**. For example, the reciprocal of $\frac{5}{8}$ is $\frac{8}{5}$. The reciprocal of 2 is $\frac{1}{2}$.

Remainder

The **remainder** is the number that's left over after division. The remainder when you divide 35 by 8 is 3.

Square Root

Remember this magical symbol: $\sqrt{\ }$? It indicates the **square root** of a number. So $\sqrt{16} = 4$ or -4, because both $(4)^2$ and $(-4)^2 = 16$.

You cannot add square roots unless they have a common root (the number or term under the square root sign). So you can determine that $\sqrt{2} + \sqrt{2} = 2\sqrt{2}$, because the numbers under the radicals are the same, but you can't add $\sqrt{2} + \sqrt{3}$ because the radicals are different. To multiply or divide square roots, just treat them as regular integers: $\sqrt{6} \times \sqrt{3} = \sqrt{18}$, or $3\sqrt{2}$. Basically, they're subject to the same rules as exponents. In fact, a square root is an exponent: $x^{\frac{1}{2}}$ is just $\sqrt{x}$.

Sum

The result of addition is called the **sum**.

Whole Number

A **whole number** is a number that does not have any fractional or decimal parts. The number 2 is a whole number, but 2.5 is not.

Zero

Zero is an integer; it's neither positive nor negative, and it's even. Multiplying by 0 always results in a product of 0, and dividing by zero is impossible.

STEP 3
Arguments

Consider this statement: "Buy American cars, because they're better. They're made by American workers." The author of the statement is trying to convince you of something, right? His point is that you should buy an American car, and the reason he gives in support of this point is that American cars are better because Americans make them. To refute his argument, you could give an example of a better way of determining what makes a car superior, or you could present a case in which a product made by American workers is inferior.

On the GMAT, statements like the one above are followed by a question and five answer choices. GMAC calls this type of question "critical reasoning," but we call it an argument. Why? Well, each problem contains a paragraph, within which the author states a point and argues it with facts.

One-third of your GMAT Verbal section (about 14 questions) will be arguments. Take a closer look at the argument below:

> *Although fresh oats and corn are the most nutritious foods for cattle, historically, cattle ranchers have minimized purchases of these grains in order to minimize costs due to spoilage. This year, however, fresh oats and corn have become the best-selling foods for cattle—a clear sign that cattle ranchers are putting nutrition ahead of concerns about costs due to spoilage.*

Which of the following, if true, most seriously weakens the argument above?

○ Last year, processed cattle feed outsold fresh oats and corn by a wide margin.

○ No cattle ranchers have reported in surveys that they are attempting to purchase more nutritious fodder for their herds.

○ Cattle ranchers are attempting to counter recent claims about the health risks associated with eating beef by becoming more conscious of the nutritive quality of the meat they are producing.

○ Because of crop failures, all types of cattle fodder—including fresh oats and corn, processed cattle feed, and frozen nutritional supplements—were more expensive this year than in previous years.

○ Because of agricultural innovations, fresh oats and corn spoil much less quickly than in previous years, while the purchase price for such fodder has remained constant.

If you're like most people, you raced through the argument, glanced at the question, and went straight to the answer choices. You may have even jumped back and forth several times from the passage to the answer choices, wasting time, and perhaps not even ending up with the best answer. There's a better way to tackle these argument problems.

The Four-Step Approach

It doesn't do much good to read the argument before you know what you're looking for. In our Four-Step Approach, you read the question first so you know what sorts of things to look for. You start by answering the questions in your own words, and by aggressively using POE to eliminate wrong answer choices. To introduce you to the Four-Step Approach, we'll work through the argument above together.

Step 1: Read the Question

Yes, that's right. Skip over the argument entirely and go straight to the question. Why? Because reading the question will tell you what to look for in the passage. Once you know that, you can read through the argument with a purpose, and you'll get more out of the argument by knowing what you're looking for. Here's the question again:

Which of the following, if true, most seriously weakens the argument above?

Now we know what we're looking for—a way to weaken the author's argument. We might find that the author has come to a conclusion that he does not support with facts, or we might determine that, in constructing his argument, the author has neglected to rule out other possible causes or outcomes. He may have included information in the conclusion that's unsupported or even unmentioned in the body of the argument. We may find his reasoning circular, overly general, hyperbolic, or in some other way illogical. So when we read the argument, we'll look for weak spots to attack—places in which the reasoning of the argument is flawed. That's our next step.

Step 2: Break It Down

To break down an argument, we'll first need to identify the author's main idea, or point, and then the reasons he cites to support that point. The author's point, as we mentioned above, is what he's trying to convince you of—it's the whole reason why he wrote the argument. If you have trouble determining the point, try asking yourself, "What's he trying to say? If he were writing a TV commercial, what would he be selling? If he were a politician, what would he be advocating?" The answer to any one of these questions is the author's point.

You'll also need to take note of the facts or reasons the author uses in supporting his point. Does he cite a survey? Outline a chain of cause and effect? Refer to authorities, publications, or popular opinion? Does he bring up historical evidence? We'll call each piece of evidence the author uses to support his argument a *premise*.

If you're having trouble locating the premises in the argument, try using this simple test: State the conclusion, and then ask yourself, "Why?" The information that answers the question "why?" constitutes the author's premises.

As you read, also keep an eye out for flaws or weaknesses, as discussed above. Okay, here's the argument again:

Although fresh oats and corn are the most nutritious foods for cattle, historically, cattle ranchers have minimized purchases of these grains in order to minimize costs due to spoilage. This year, however, fresh oats and corn have become the best-selling foods for cattle—a clear sign that cattle ranchers are putting nutrition ahead of concerns about costs due to spoilage.

All right. What is the author's conclusion? Go ahead and state it in your own words; and then write it on a piece of scrap paper.

You may have written something like "Cattle ranchers are putting nutrition ahead of cost concerns" or "Cattle ranchers put nutrition ahead of cost." However you stated the conclusion is fine, as long as you understood that the author is trying to convince you that cattle ranchers care more about nutrition than they do about the cost of feed.

Next, since the question tells us to weaken the author's argument, we need to examine the premises the author gave in support of his point. Ask yourself "Why does the author believe cattle ranchers are putting nutrition ahead of cost concerns?" Jot down his premises on a piece of scrap paper.

Hopefully you wrote down something like "Fresh oats and corn are the most nutritious foods for cattle. Historically, ranchers haven't purchased a lot of them because they spoil. This year fresh oats and corn were the best-selling food for cattle." It is based on the fact that oats and corn are selling so well that the author concludes that cattle ranchers are putting nutrition ahead of cost concerns.

Do you believe the author's argument, based solely on the information he gives you? Are you just going to take his word for it? No, of course not. The author has left some large gaps in the fabric of his argument, and he's relying on you to fill them in with assumptions.

Assumptions are unstated factors in an argument; often they can appear to support the conclusion. The farmer's conclusion, that ranchers are putting nutrition ahead of cost, rests on a single fact: fresh corn and oats outsold other forms of cattle feed this year, even though they have historically been more expensive. The author is depending on you to fill in the gap, to supply the missing information that will make his argument work.

What piece of information could you supply to further support the conclusion? Well, you could provide evidence that demonstrates that nutrition is the only reason cattle ranchers are buying fresh corn and oats this year, or you could rule out other reasons for this phenomenon. In any event, we will focus our attack on this weak point: the gap in his argument where the author expects you to do his work for him by filling in assumptions.

Step 3: Answer the Question in Your Own Words

Reread the question (but keep ignoring those answer choices!). It asks us how we might weaken the author's argument. Did anything strike you as incomplete about the argument as you read it? Does the author's reasoning seem sound to you? To weaken an argument, we look for flaws or gaps in the author's reasoning. If we can find another way to reach the same conclusion as the author, or if we can show that the premises the author uses to support his argument are not sound, then we are weakening the argument.

Okay, so we already established that the author expects you to assume that concern about nutrition is the sole reason cattle ranchers are buying more fresh feed. He draws his conclusion, that ranchers are putting nutrition ahead of cost concerns, based on only one piece of evidence: Fresh oats and corn have become the best-selling food for cattle. If the author were sitting right in front of you, what would you say to refute his argument? Can you think of any other reason why corn and oats might be selling better this year?

You can probably think of a few reasons, such as a higher birthrate among cattle, resulting in more stock to feed, or a lower availability of other foodstuffs. Or you might have said that previous concerns about spoilage had been alleviated, or that the price had dropped to such a degree that ranchers were more willing to risk spoilage. There are a number of possible reasons that fresh corn and oats might have become best-selling foods, besides the author's stated reason. All right—now you're ready to attack those answer choices.

Step 4: Apply Process of Elimination

Since we're going after the weak spots, or assumptions, in the argument, let's look for an answer choice that will drive a wedge between the conclusion and the premises. In fact, as you read each answer choice, you can ask yourself, "Does this weaken it?" If you answer no, eliminate it.

We'll read all five answer choices below. All you know about the fascinating topic of cattle feed is what you've been told by the argument, so make sure you keep your thinking narrow. Let's start.

○   Last year, processed cattle feed outsold
     fresh oats and corn by a wide margin.

No. We are trying to weaken the argument, so what happened last year does not matter. We want to know what happened this year. Eliminate this answer choice.

○   No cattle ranchers have reported in
     surveys that they are attempting to
     purchase more nutritious fodder for
     their herds.

No. This answer choice actually argues against the conclusion, which is (perhaps surprisingly) never a valid way to weaken an argument. All you do when you argue against the conclusion is set up another line of reasoning that might be just as flawed as the original argument. In this case, for instance, there are all kinds of problems with the validity of surveys, and that alone makes this attack particularly weak. We're better off attacking the issue of whether or not large corn and oat purchases signal that ranchers value nutrition more highly than cost savings.

○   Cattle ranchers are attempting to
     counter recent claims about the health
     risks associated with eating beef by
     becoming more conscious of the
     nutritive quality of the meat they are
     producing.

No. This answer choice, in fact, strengthens the position that nutrition is the sole reason cattle ranchers have increased their purchases of fresh fodder. Remember that we're trying to weaken the argument by citing a reason (besides nutrition) that cattle ranchers are buying different feed this year. Eliminate it.

○ Because of crop failures, all types of
cattle fodder—including fresh oats and
corn, processed cattle feed, and frozen
nutritional supplements—were more
expensive this year than in previous
years.

No. Though this answer choice states that all types of feed are more expensive, it doesn't tell us that the cost of fresh oats and corn was surpassed in cost by the other feeds. It is more likely that oats and corn are still proportionally more expensive than the other feeds. This answer choice doesn't tell us anything about nutrition either, so this doesn't help us weaken the argument. Eliminate it.

○ Because of agricultural innovations, fresh
oats and corn spoil much less quickly
than in previous years, while the
purchase price for such fodder has
remained constant.

Okay, that sounds more like it. Now that corn and oats do not spoil as quickly, costs (related to spoilage) are lower. Ranchers may or may not value nutrition more highly than monetary savings, but the costs associated with corn and oats have decreased. Cost is no longer a barrier to buying better food, and finally we have a reason, besides nutrition, that cattle ranchers are buying fresh fodder.

So, choice (E) is the correct answer. Even if we didn't immediately see why (E) was what we were looking for, we would have picked it anyway because there was something provably wrong with the other four answer choices.

More on Process of Elimination (POE)

By using the Four-Step Approach, you determined that choice (E) was the best answer to the question above. But maybe you're not so sure whether, left on your own, you'd have seen clear reasons for eliminating those four answer choices. So let's take a closer look at some common reasons for eliminating answer choices in POE.

Scope

You will succeed on arguments only if you are able to keep your focus very narrow. Remember that all you know about the topic in question is what you were told in that paragraph. Put simply, the *scope* of the argument is dictated by the information given in the conclusion and the premises.

With this in mind, let's take another look at answer choice (A). The scope of the cattle feed argument is confined to what has taken place this year, so information about last year is beyond the argument's scope. When you see an answer choice that goes beyond the realm of the argument, you can consider it *out of scope* and eliminate it. Scope is by far the most common reason for eliminating answer choices in the arguments section.

Opposite

When you're dealing with questions that ask you to weaken or strengthen the author's conclusion, be very wary of answer choices that, while within the scope, do exactly the opposite of what you want. Answer choice (C) is a prime example of this. You're looking for a reason, aside from nutrition, to explain why ranchers are buying more fresh feed this year, but answer choice (C) simply gives yet another way in which nutrition is the sole motivational factor. Thus, while it is in the scope of the argument, it is the opposite of the answer choice you want, and you should eliminate it.

Extreme

Extreme wording is another very common reason for eliminating answer choices in POE. Extreme statements, such as "Everybody loves Picasso," can be easily disproved. This, therefore, is not the type of answer choice GMAC is likely to count as the credited response.

Go ahead and try the following question. Work through your Four-Step Approach on this question, paying special attention to POE when you get to the answer choices.

To many environmentalists, the extinction of plants—accompanied by the increasing genetic uniformity of food crops—is the single most serious environmental problem. Something must be done to prevent the loss of wild food plants or no-longer-cultivated food plants. Otherwise, the lack of genetic food diversity could allow for significant portions of major crops to be destroyed overnight. In 1970, for example, southern leaf blight destroyed approximately 20 percent of the United States corn crop, leaving very few varieties of corn unaffected, in the areas over which the disease spread.

Which of the following can be inferred from the passage above?

○   Susceptibility to certain plant diseases is genetically determined.

○   Eighty percent of the corn grown in the United States is completely resistant to southern leaf blight.

○   The extinction of wild food plants can be traced back definitively to destructive plant diseases.

○   Plant breeders must focus on developing plants that are resistant to plant disease.

○   Corn is the only food crop threatened by southern leaf blight.

Step 1:   **Read the Question.** This question is an example of a type of question we call Inference. Much like the Inference questions in reading comprehension portions of the test, these questions ask you not to deduce, but to actually *point to* something in the passage.

Step 2:   **Break It Down.** Since arguments with Inference questions have an extremely narrow scope, read them even more closely than you usually would. As you break down the argument in these types of questions, you may or may not find an actual point. Focus instead on the scope of the argument, the facts presented, and how they fit together.

Step 3: Answer the Question in Your Own Words. Because Inference questions hinge on what you know to be true from the facts in the argument, it is hard to anticipate what a good answer choice will look like, or even to state the answer in your own words. But the understanding you gained of the argument's scope and supporting facts will be enough to get you through your POE.

Step 4: Apply Process of Elimination. You will need to read each answer choice very closely, keeping in mind that the only thing you know about corn, food crops, and southern leaf blight is what you've read in the argument. When eliminating answer choices, ask yourself, "Do I know this?" If you cannot actually point to the information from the answer choice somewhere in the argument, you should eliminate it. Also eliminate answer choices that are outside the scope of the argument or that contain extreme wording.

In the preceding argument, the scope is a very narrow discussion of the causes of destruction of food crops. Although the first sentence sets the stage for the topic, it does little more than that. The argument presents a concern about a lack of genetic food diversity and its effect on the long-term health of food crops. An example about the southern leaf blight of 1970 is presented to strengthen the argument.

Keeping that in mind, let's look through the answer choices.

○ Susceptibility to certain plant diseases is genetically determined.

Well, maybe. The argument does say, "the lack of genetic diversity could allow a significant portion of a major crop to be destroyed overnight." It isn't great, but we'll keep this answer choice for now.

○ Eighty percent of the corn grown in the United States is completely resistant to southern leaf blight.

No. There are a couple of reasons that this answer choice is no good. First of all, we cannot possibly know that a crop is completely resistant to southern leaf blight. *Completely* is an example of the kind of extreme wording that allows us to eliminate an answer choice. Furthermore, watch out for traps like this one: Just because you know that 20 percent of the U.S. corn crop was destroyed in 1970 doesn't mean that the 80 percent remaining was resistant. Eliminate it.

> ○ The extinction of wild food plants can
> be traced back definitively to destructive
> plant diseases.

No. Again, watch out for extreme wording. Do we know that this is true in all cases, based on the facts in the argument? No, we don't. As we mentioned, extreme wording like this needs only one counterexample to prove it false, so this is the kind of answer choice GMAC will not credit. Eliminate it.

> ○ Plant breeders must focus on developing
> plants that are resistant to plant disease.

No. What plant breeders actually do is outside the scope of the argument—the argument states only that "Something must be done..." Also, watch out for that extreme wording—answer choices that predict the future or mandate a course of action are too extreme to be the credited response. Eliminate it.

> ○ Corn is the only food crop threatened by
> southern leaf blight.

No. Isn't it extreme to say that corn was the *only* plant threatened by southern leaf blight? We know that corn was affected, but we don't know if the other plants on the planet were, so eliminate it.

This leaves us with choice (A). Admittedly, not the most flashy or exciting thing about the argument, but definitely something we can point to as true. This is the way Inference questions typically work—you'll have to rely heavily on POE, because the best answer rarely jumps out at you; it's most often just an incidental fact or paraphrase.

Taking POE One Step Further

POE works extremely well in helping you narrow down the answer choices. Often, you'll even be able to eliminate three of the choices right away using POE, and will be left with two that seem very similar. To avoid having to desperately guess, when you're so close to the credited response, we'll now refine our POE so it can help you discern between even two answer choices that may seem very similar.

Down to Two Answers

If you tend to find yourself stumped or stalled after having eliminated three answer choices, try this:

Read each remaining choice and concentrate on finding the difference between them. There may be a word, a phrase, or an entire idea that you missed the first time through. Use this difference to determine which answer choice to eliminate, and refer to the argument if necessary.

Okay, so now try using your Four-Step Approach on the following question:

> Between 1986 and 1991, the restaurant industry saw an average table occupancy rate (i.e., percent of the time that a table was occupied) of 74 percent, while the number of meals eaten out by Americans stayed constant, at an average of 212 meals out per month per 1,000 people. Between 1991 and 1996, however, the average table occupancy rose to 81 percent, while the number of meals eaten by Americans declined to 195 meals out per month per 1,000 people.

Which of the following most contributes to an explanation of the discrepancy between the average table occupancy and the number of meals eaten out in the period between 1991 and 1996?

○ The average amount of time spent per meal by Americans eating out increased between 1991 and 1996.

○ The proportion of very lengthy meals to somewhat lengthy meals was greater in 1996 than in 1986.

○ The average number of Americans dining out per month tends to decline whenever table occupancy rates increase.

○ The number of meals served between 1986 and 1991 was fewer than the number of meals served between 1991 and 1996.

○ The more tables a restaurant has, the higher its occupancy rate is likely to be.

Step 1: Read the Question. The question asked you to explain a discrepancy in the facts presented by the argument. We call this type of question "Resolve the Paradox." As you read the argument, keep an eye out for facts that are at odds with each other.

Step 2: Break It Down. Paraphrase the discrepancy in the argument. Here's a hint: You will find it on both sides of a conjunction like *however*.

Step 3: Answer the Question in Your Own Words. The scope of a discrepancy or Paradox argument is very narrow—it's usually just the discrepant facts and a detail that might reconcile them. Think about what facts or information would link the disparate facts in the argument. If you know what you're looking for in advance, you'll be more likely to recognize it when you see it.

Step 4: Apply Process of Elimination. Try this on your own. Okay, you probably eliminated (C) because it is too broad and (E) because it is out of scope. Additionally, both answer choices rely on information that's not furnished in the argument. You may also have eliminated (D) because the number of meals served does not affect why the average table occupancy rate went up.

So you're left with choices (A) and (B), which, at first glance, seem very similar. But take a closer look at the two answer choices. Both discuss the length of time per meal, but they differ in that choice (A) talks about the average time per meal, while (B) refers to "very lengthy" versus "somewhat lengthy" meals. Take a closer look at (B) in light of the information presented in the argument. You'll see that nowhere do we find a way to differentiate between "somewhat lengthy" and "very lengthy" meals. We can say only that meals in general must have been longer, which is the information given in answer choice (A).

More Question Types

The questions on the GMAT fall into predictable patterns; certain *types* of arguments appear again and again on the test. Therefore, you can learn how to identify and solve them using the Four-Step Approach. Up to this point, you have already seen three common argument types—weaken, inference, and paradox—and now we'll look at the three that remain: strengthen, assumption, and reasoning.

Strengthen

You've already seen a question in which you were asked to weaken the author's argument, and you did this by attacking a weak spot in the argument, where the test writers expect you to assume something.

The approach to strengthen questions is similar, but instead of attacking the argument at its weakest point, you'll provide additional information to strengthen the weak point. So, if the author proves his point by making an assumption, you'll include additional data to bolster the assumption. If the author cites a survey in support of his conclusion, you'll give evidence to prove the validity of the survey. If the author draws his conclusion by means of a comparison, you'll cite further similarities to make the analogy stronger.

The most common structure for arguments you'll be asked to strengthen (or weaken) is one in which assumptions are based on a causal link. The underlying assumptions in a causal argument are that the stated cause is directly responsible for the outcome, and that there is no other cause. Let's take a look at an argument of this type.

A recent article in a prominent medical journal examines rates of colon cancer among both male and female members of the population. The author, a well-respected cancer researcher, found that while the majority of colon cancer sufferers are female, the majority of test subjects in clinical trials on colon cancer medication and treatment are male. Specifically, her research revealed that while the ratio of male test subjects to female test subjects was three to one, women are, in fact, more than twice as likely to be diagnosed with colon cancer than men. The researcher concludes that "Women experience a higher incidence of colon cancer than their male counterparts. This is due to an overreliance in medical research on male test subjects."

The author's conclusion, that women have a higher likelihood of contracting colon cancer than men, is supported mainly by the premise, "while the majority of colon cancer sufferers are female, the majority of test subjects in clinical trials on colon cancer medication and treatment are male." The author states no other cause for the higher incidence of colon cancer among women, and in fact, the conclusion of this argument can be supported only if we assume that the ratio of male to female test subjects alone is enough to cause the higher incidence of colon cancer among females.

An argument like this is weak because its conclusion depends on a causal link. Its assumptions are that (a) the cause is directly responsible for the effect, and (b) nothing else contributes to or is causing the outcome. The cancer researcher's argument can work only if you assume that (a) the higher incidence of colon cancer in women is caused by the ratio of male to female test subjects, and that (b) nothing else causes this higher incidence of colon cancer among women.

To strengthen an argument like this one, you need to give the assumptions additional support, either by reinforcing the causal link or by discounting alternate causes. A credited response for the argument above might read, "Diagnostic techniques do not differ from men to women, and women are equally as likely to report symptoms that lead to diagnosis as men." In this way, we rule out the possibility that more women seek treatment or that women are more likely to be diagnosed due to a difference in the technology.

Assumption

Another common argument type is one that asks you to identify the underlying assumptions of the argument, or evaluate how each answer choice contributes to the support of the conclusion. In these cases, the best answer is one that states the unspoken assumption in the argument, while staying within the argument's scope. Work through the following argument, using the Four-Step Approach.

> Serious novelists start writing because of a desire to create a work of art, and therefore they recognize as great literature the works of other novelists who achieve this goal. As a consequence, when a novel becomes a bestseller, the authors of other novels conclude that the bestseller is not truly great literature.

> The explanation offered above for the view authors hold of bestsellers assumes that

- ○ work on a novel that the author hopes will be regarded as great literature must be undertaken in solitude
- ○ serious novelists tend not to view as great literature a novel produced by an author whose success they envy
- ○ a novelist can produce a bestseller without having already produced great literature
- ○ serious novelists believe that those novelists who produce bestsellers must not have aimed at producing a work of art
- ○ the claim of a novel to status as great literature cannot be evaluated by individuals who are not themselves serious novelists

The correct answer is choice (D). The question asks us to state an assumption of the argument. The conclusion of the argument is that when a novel becomes a bestseller, other authors do not regard it as great literature. The premise is that serious novelists write because of a desire to create a work of art, and the argument assumes that one cannot simultaneously create a work of art and a bestseller.

Answer choices (A) and (B) are out of the scope of the argument; we are told nothing about solitude or envy. Choice (C) is also out of the scope; we are not talking about the entire works of an author, but one book. Furthermore, we are not looking to support the argument. Answer choice (E) is also out of scope; the argument is concerned with books that become bestsellers, and not those that become great literature. This leaves (D), which is the assumption we were looking for.

Reasoning

The last and least common type of argument is one that deals not with the content of the argument, but with how it is structured. Questions of this type may read as follows:

> Which of the following indicates a flaw in the reasoning above?
>
> Susan's attempt to counter Tim's claim is best characterized as...
>
> Dan's response has which of the following relationships to Alissa's argument?
>
> The author makes his point chiefly by...

Your Four-Step Approach works on arguments of this type as well. The major difference here is that with a reasoning question, as you break it down and state the answer in your own words, you will focus more on describing the pattern of reasoning than in paraphrasing the content of the argument. Try the following question:

TIM: When a rare tragedy, such as a plane crash, occurs, many people profess a belief that they themselves are more likely to experience such a tragedy and take extraordinary measures to prevent it. This is unfounded, however. Winning a lottery jackpot, an extremely rare event, does not mean you are any more likely to win a second time.

SUSAN: I disagree. The belief is well founded. People who sense danger are more likely to trust their instincts and act in such a way as to prevent the danger from befalling them.

Susan's attempt to counter Tim's argument is best characterized as one that

○ makes apparent Tim's failure to consider the consequences of such a tragedy to its survivors

○ challenges Tim's assumption that the occurrence of a single event is sufficient to predict future occurrences of that event

○ questions the appropriateness of the analogy drawn by Tim

○ presents an alternate basis for judging the validity of people's reactions

○ disputes the meaning of the term *unfounded*

How'd you do? The question asks you to characterize the argument and is, therefore, a reasoning question—it's more concerned with structure than content. As you break it down, take note of the way Susan fails to address Tim's premise, but instead introduces her own reasoning. In this case, Tim describes behavior in response to a tragedy, and dismisses it as "unfounded" based on his lottery analogy. Susan provides an alternate explanation for people's behavior. As you use Process of Elimination, ask yourself, "Did they do that?" as a way of testing each answer choice.

Here we go:

    (A)   No. Neither of them discusses the effect of tragedy on its survivors. Eliminate it.

    (B)   No. Susan does not even address Tim's assumption about the frequency or likelihood of the recurrence of such an event in the future. Eliminate it.

    (C)   No. Susan does not speak about Tim's analogy. Eliminate it.

    (D)   Yes. Susan presents another explanation for the behavior pointed out by Tim— that people are more likely to trust their instincts and possibly avert misfortune.

    (E)   No. There is no such dispute in Susan's argument. Eliminate it.

STEP 4

Algebra and Its Alternatives

The Quantitative section on the GMAT involves an awful lot of what looks like algebra. You can avoid most of the algebra you encounter though, or at least reduce the work you have to do by employing POE or by Plugging In. Plugging In is a technique for turning an algebra problem into a plain arithmetic problem. Intrigued? We'll get to Plugging In shortly, but first we have a little business to get out of the way.

Solving for x

You can solve any equation that contains only one variable by *manipulating the equation*. This means that through a series of basic arithmetic steps, you move all the numerical terms to one side of the equation, isolating the variable on the other side. The most important thing to remember here is that you must treat both sides of the equation the same: If you subtract 3 from one side, you must subtract it from the other.

Let's take a look at the following example:

$$3x + 4 = 10$$

Your goal is to isolate the variable x on one side of the equal sign; start by getting all the numbers together. On the left, you have +4, so subtract 4 from both sides:

$$3x + 4 = 10$$

$$3x = 10 - 4$$

$$3x = 6$$

Hopefully you can look at this and recognize that $x = 2$, but the final step is to divide both sides by 3.

$$\frac{3x}{3} = \frac{6}{3}, x = 2$$

Nicely done! And now, when you encounter plain equations with variables, you'll know exactly what to do. But occasionally you'll see a word problem, which means you'll have to set up your own equation. Let's start by taking a look at problems dealing with percents, which commonly require you to write your own equation.

Percents

Percent means "out of 100." If 82 percent of the population has Type O blood, then 82 "out of 100" people have Type O blood. A quarter is 25 cents, also known as $\frac{25}{100}$, or 25 percent of a dollar. Since many of the GMAT problems about percents are word problems, you'll have to start by translating the English into math so that you can solve them. Here's an example:

> Susan spends 40 percent of her salary (after taxes) on rent each month. If she's paid $48,000 per year (after taxes), how much does Susan spend on rent each month?

Susan's salary is $48,000 per year, but she pays her rent by the month. We need to determine what percent of her monthly salary is paid in rent. Susan's monthly salary is $\frac{48,000}{12}$, or $4,000 per month.

To figure out the amount Susan pays in rent, ask yourself *What is 40 percent of $4,000?* Once you have this, you can turn the question into an equation and solve. Take a look at the translation table below:

English	Translates
What	x
Is	$=$
Percent	$\left(\frac{1}{100}\right)$
Of	$\times$

What is 40 percent of $4,000 becomes $x = 40 \left(\dfrac{1}{100} \right) \times 4{,}000$.

Now solve for x:

$$x = \frac{40}{100} \times 4{,}000$$

$$x = \frac{4}{10} \times 4{,}000$$

$$x = \frac{4 \times 4{,}000}{10}$$

$$x = \frac{4 \times 400}{1}$$

$$x = 1{,}600$$

Susan spends $1,600 per month on rent.

Percent Change

A special category of percent problems on the GMAT asks about the percentage amount by which something has increased or decreased. To answer these types of questions, use the following formula:

$$\text{Percent Change} = \frac{\text{difference}}{\text{original}} \times 100$$

The advantage of this formula is that there are only two questions you have to ask yourself: What's the difference? And what's the original? Let's try an example:

> An art dealer recently raised the price of a painting from $5,000 to $6,000. By what percent did she raise the price?
>
> ○ 10%
> ○ 20%
> ○ 25%
> ○ 100%
> ○ 1,000%

Okay. Answer the first question: What's the difference?

$6,000 – $5,000 = $1,000. So that's the difference.

Now, answer the second question: What's the original?

The price went *from* $5,000 to $6,000, so the original price was $5,000.

Use the formula:

$$\frac{1,000}{5,000} \times 100 = \frac{1}{5} \times 100 = 20\%$$

So, the price increased by 20%, and the correct answer is (B).

Plugging In

You'll see many word problems on the GMAT that look as though you'll need to write out a series of algebraic equations in order to solve them. The good news is you don't have to. You can turn algebra into arithmetic by using the Plugging In method.

Consider the following question:

> Martin has *s* marbles more than Keith does, and *p* fewer than George. If Martin has *m* marbles, how many marbles do Keith and George have in terms of *m, s,* and *p* ?
>
> ○ $m + s + p$
> ○ $m - s + p$
> ○ $3m - s + p$
> ○ $2m - s + p$
> ○ $3m + s - p$

Wouldn't this problem be easier if you just *knew* how many marbles Martin had? Well, since the entire problem is algebraic, the relationship between the number of marbles Martin has and the number of marbles Keith has will always be the same—if Martin has 10 marbles, Keith will have 10 – *s*. Let's try just assuming that Martin *does* have 10 marbles, and see what happens.

Give Martin 10 marbles. He has s more than Keith, so let's say $s = 3$ and Martin has 3 more than Keith. Why 3? Why not? So Keith has 7 marbles. Now, p fewer than George? How about 5 fewer than George, so George has 15.

Now let's answer the question. How many marbles do Keith and George have together? Keith has 7 and George has 15, so together they have 22.

But what about those algebraic answer choices? Simple, just plug in the numbers you used in the problem in place of the variables. So plug in 10 for m, 3 for s, and 5 for p. When you find an answer choice that equals 22 marbles, that's it. Check them all to be safe.

(A) $m + s + p$

      $10 + 3 + 5$

That isn't 22. Keep going.

(B) $m - s + p$

      $10 - 3 + 5$

That isn't 22. Keep going.

(C) $3m - s + p$

      $3(10) - 3 + 5$

      $30 + 2$

That isn't 22 either. Keep going.

(D) $2m - s + p$

      $2(10) - 3 + 5$

      $20 + 2$

Yep. That's 22. You have a winner.

(E) $3m + s - p$

      $3(10) + 3 - 5$

And that one isn't 22 either.

So you've turned a nasty algebraic word problem into a simple arithmetic one. Let's recap the steps for Plugging In:

- Replace all the variables in the problem with numbers.

- Read through the new problem and answer the question.

- Plug your numbers into the answer choices and look for your number.

Here Are a Couple of Other Important Thoughts on Basic Plugging In:

Write everything down. Carefully write everything down on your noteboard—you need to write down what every variable equals, what every part of the problem equals, and what your answer is. Rewrite every answer choice with your numbers—don't solve in your head.

Plug in friendly numbers. Why plug in ugly numbers that will only make the arithmetic difficult? For example, if a question asks for the price of something, make it $100, because $100 is easy to work with. In questions about time, plug in 30 or 60 for the number of seconds or minutes. You get the picture.

Practice makes perfect. Plugging In works even on easy algebraic word problems, and if you don't practice using it on the easy ones, it won't work for you on the hard ones.

How to Spot a Plugging In Problem

Plugging In problems come in many shapes and sizes. The most common type is a word problem in which you have variables in both the question and the answer choices, as in the problem above. Two other types of Plugging In problems are the "Hidden" Plug In problem and the "Must Be" problem. The following examples will show you what we mean.

Hidden Plug In

Take a look at the following example of a Plugging In problem where the variable is "hidden," meaning that it is not marked by a letter such as *x* or *y*. Instead, this type of Plugging In problem contains a piece of information that is missing, and that information is needed to solve the problem.

> In 2015, Ashley invited 12% more people to her annual celebration than she did in 2014. If every subsequent year Ashley invites 10% more people to her annual celebration than she did the year before, then the number of people she invites in 2017 is approximately what percentage greater than the number of people she invited in 2014 ?
>
> ○   22%
> ○   32%
> ○   35%
> ○   48%
> ○   135%

There is an important piece of information missing from this question, so identify what that is and plug in a number for it. The question wants to know what percentage greater the number of people invited to the annual celebration was in 2017 than 2014. It is helpful to know number of people invited in 2014 to answer this question, so Plug In. Since the problem deals with percentages, plug in 100 for the number of people invited in 2014. In 2015, Ashley invites 12% more people, so the number of people invited in 2015 is $100 \times 1.12 = 112$. She invites 10% more people in every subsequent year than she did the year before, so in 2016, she invited 10% more than 112, which is $112 \times 1.10 = 123.2$. In 2017 she invited 10% more than 123.2, so she invited $123.2 \times 1.10 = 135.52$ people.

Now, figure out what percent greater 135.52 is than 100 by using the percent change formula, which is $\frac{difference}{original} \times 100$. The difference is $135.52 - 100 = 35.52$, and the original is 100, so the percent change is $\dfrac{35.52}{100} \times 100 = 35.52\%$. Therefore, the correct answer is choice (C), 35%.

Must Be

Here's an example of a "Must Be" problem.

> If x and y are consecutive integers and $x < y$, then $y^2 - x^2$ must be
>
> ○   a prime number
> ○   an odd number
> ○   an even number
> ○   the square of an integer
> ○   equivalent to $(y - x)^2$

The question asks you what *must* be true. You should plug in on a question like this, but the important difference here is that you'll need to plug in two times. Here's why.

Let $x = 2$ and $y = 3$; then plug them into the equation $y^2 - x^2$. This gives you 9 – 4, which equals 5. But when you go to the answer choices, you'll see that 5 could make the answer either (A) a prime number or (B) an odd number, so you need to plug in again to eliminate one of those two answer choices. For now, cross out answer choices (C), (D), and (E).

Choose two more numbers, like $x = 4$ and $y = 5$. $y^2 - x^2$ is 25 – 16, which is 9. Since 9 is an odd number, but it's not prime, you can safely choose (B). When you plug in the second time, remember to check only the two answer choices you have left!

Data Sufficiency

Roughly half of the math problems on the GMAT won't require you to do any problem solving at all. That's good news, right? Data sufficiency is confusing to many mainly because the concept is hard to get used to, and also because data sufficiency requires a very systematic approach.

In data sufficiency questions, the directions are more confusing than the actual problems, but we'll show you how to easily understand what the answer choices mean.

Before we proceed into the more sophisticated types of data sufficiency questions, let's get a handle on those directions. We'll work through a simple example:

> What is the value of x ?
> (1) $2x = 14$
> (2) $x + y = 10$

Every data sufficiency problem consists of a question followed by two statements. You have to decide NOT what the answer is, but WHETHER the question can be answered based on the information in the two statements. There are five possible answers, and they are always the same:

- ○ Statement (1) ALONE is sufficient, but statement (2) alone is not sufficient.
- ○ Statement (2) ALONE is sufficient, but statement (1) alone is not sufficient.
- ○ BOTH statements TOGETHER are sufficient, but NEITHER statement ALONE is sufficient.
- ○ EACH statement ALONE is sufficient.
- ○ Statements (1) and (2) TOGETHER are not sufficient.

The fundamental question of data sufficiency is "Does this statement tell me enough that I can answer the question?" And it is absolutely critical that you begin by considering one statement at a time.

Start with statement (1) and ignore statement (2). Statement (1) tells us that $2x = 14$. Does this tell us enough to answer the question "What is the value of x?" Yes it does, so statement (1) is sufficient. This means that, of all the answer choices, only choice (A) "statement (1) alone is sufficient" and choice (D) "statement (1) alone and statement (2) alone are sufficient" are possible answers. Write down all five answer choices on your noteboard and cross out choices (B), (C), and (E).

Now consider statement (2) and ignore statement (1). Does statement (2), $x + y = 10$, tell us enough to answer the question "What is the value of x?" No, it does not. So statement (2) alone is *not* sufficient and the answer cannot be (D); it can be only (A).

AD vs. BCE

Here's a good procedure for solving data sufficiency questions:

Consider statement (1) alone. It will be either sufficient or not sufficient.

If statement (1) is sufficient, proceed as follows:

1. Write down AD.
2. Consider statement (2) alone.
    a. If statement (2) is sufficient, choose (D).
    b. If statement (2) is not sufficient, choose (A).

If statement (1) is not sufficient, proceed as follows:

1. Write down BCE.
2. Consider statement (2) alone.
    a. If statement (2) is sufficient, choose (B).
    b. If statement (2) is not sufficient, cross off (B) and consider statements (1) and (2) together.
        (1) If (1) and (2) together are sufficient, choose (C).
        (2) If (1) and (2) together are not sufficient, choose (E).

Don't Solve

Now that we have the directions under control, let's think about data sufficiency questions and what they're actually asking you to do. You'll see data sufficiency questions that ask you about the same topics as the more traditional problem-solving math questions—averages, probabilities, coordinate geometry, and the like. But there is one important difference: *You do not need to solve data sufficiency questions*. Solving data sufficiency questions wastes time and doesn't help you answer them.

Remember our example above, "What is the value of *x*?" We don't actually care what the value of *x* is, because we don't get any credit for knowing that value; we get credit only for determining whether the data in the statements are sufficient to determine the answer. Many people waste time *solving* data sufficiency questions and ruin their pacing on the Quantitative section.

The other odd thing about data sufficiency questions is that your information comes in two or three parts. The question may give you part of an equation, and each statement may provide you with another part. You have to be resourceful enough to figure out where to get the information you need. Take a look at this example:

> If a certain seamstress in a garment shop made 65 coats, what percent of the shop's total output of coats did she make?
>
> (1)   The shop made a total of 325 coats.
>
> (2)   The number of coats made by the seamstress represents $\frac{1}{5}$ of the shop's output of coats.
>
> ○   Statement (1) ALONE is sufficient, but statement (2) alone is not sufficient.
> ○   Statement (2) ALONE is sufficient, but statement (1) alone is not sufficient.
> ○   BOTH statements TOGETHER are sufficient, but NEITHER statement ALONE is sufficient.
> ○   EACH statement ALONE is sufficient.
> ○   Statements (1) and (2) TOGETHER are not sufficient.

Okay, so based on the question, and using your English-to-math translation table, you'd turn 65 is *what percent of the shop's output?* into $65 = x\left(\dfrac{1}{100}\right) \times$ *the shop's output.* You already have one variable; it's the one that answers the question what percentage, but you're missing the information about the shop's output. Consider statement (1): It tells you that the shop made 325 coats. Now you have the total and you can proceed with your equation: $65 = x\left(\dfrac{1}{100}\right) \times 325$. That's enough. You know you c*an* solve; you don't have to go ahead and do it.

At this point, you should have written AD on your noteboard. Consider statement (2) and start with your original equation: $65 = x\left(\dfrac{1}{100}\right) \times$ *the shop's output.* Statement (2) tells you that the number of coats made by the seamstress is $\dfrac{1}{5}$ of the shop's output. You can figure out the shop's output, and then plug that into the equation $65 = x\left(\dfrac{1}{100}\right) \times$ *the shop's output,* or you can stop and reason for a moment. If the seamstress made $\dfrac{1}{5}$ of all the coats put out by the shop, then you have your answer. $\dfrac{1}{5} = 20\%$, so statement (2) is sufficient. Therefore, the answer is (D). Don't get so wound up in the layers of data sufficiency questions that you forget to stop and think things out.

What?!?!?!

Some data sufficiency statements are as straightforward as $2x = 14$, while others might as well be written in a foreign language. What if you saw a problem like the following one:

How many desserts did the caterer serve?

(1) The caterer served 3 ice cream dishes and 4 cakes, and nothing else.

(2) Es gibt funf struedelen im dem kulschrank.

○ Statement (1) ALONE is sufficient, but statement (2) alone is not sufficient.

○ Statement (2) ALONE is sufficient, but statement (1) alone is not sufficient.

○ BOTH statements TOGETHER are sufficient, but NEITHER statement ALONE is sufficient

○ EACH statement ALONE is sufficient.

○ Statements (1) and (2) TOGETHER are not sufficient.

Well, starting with statement (1) allows you to narrow the answer choices down to AD. What if you have absolutely no idea what statement (2) is saying? That's okay. Even though you cannot decipher statement (2), you still have a 50 percent shot, so guess (A) or (D) and go on.

Plugging In on Data Sufficiency

You can (and absolutely should) plug in on data sufficiency questions, but be careful. You may have to plug in more than once. Let's look at the following question:

Is $\frac{x}{2}$ an integer?

(1) $2x$ is an even integer.
(2) $2x = 3$

○ Statement (1) ALONE is sufficient, but statement (2) alone is not sufficient.
○ Statement (2) ALONE is sufficient, but statement (1) alone is not sufficient.
○ BOTH statements TOGETHER are sufficient, but NEITHER statement ALONE is sufficient.
○ EACH statement ALONE is sufficient.
○ Statements (1) and (2) TOGETHER are not sufficient.

The question is not asking what the value of $\frac{x}{2}$ is; it's just asking whether $\frac{x}{2}$ is an integer. And whether the answer is yes or no, as long as you can answer definitively one way or the other, the data are sufficient.

Start with statement (1), and plug in. You must plug in values that make the statement true. For example, you can plug in 2 for x in statement (1), because $2x$ is 4 and that's an even integer. But you cannot plug in $\frac{2}{3}$, because $2\left(\frac{2}{3}\right)$ is not an integer. Now, since 2 is okay for x in statement (1), plug 2 into the question and see what happens.

$$\frac{x}{2} = \frac{2}{2} = 1$$

That's an integer, so the answer is *yes*. But is the answer *always* yes? Try another number, like 3. We can test statement (1) using 3, because statement (1) stipulates that $2x$ is an integer, and with 3 for x, $2x$ is an integer; it's 6. But when you plug in 3 for x in the question, you get $\frac{x}{2}$, and $\frac{3}{2}$ is not an integer, so the answer is no. This means that statement (1) is not sufficient—Plugging In different numbers gives you different answers.

Write down BCE and move on to statement (2), which tells you that $2x = 3$. So x can only be $\frac{3}{2}$. No need to plug in here. If x is $\frac{3}{2}$, then you can answer the question Is $\frac{x}{2}$ an *integer*? Statement (2) alone is sufficient and the answer is (B).

Formulas

There are certain math concepts that GMAC loves to test repeatedly. You probably learned these concepts back in high school, but you may have forgotten them entirely. After all, when was the last time you found the mode of anything? We've simplified each of these concepts down to a formula or a clear-cut, systematic approach that you should memorize or familiarize yourself with. By learning these concepts, you'll be able to deal with averages, rate problems, and even probabilities, no matter how cleverly GMAC disguises them.

Distance

Flash back to high school. Remember those dreaded word problems in which train A left the station at 6 P.M. traveling 70 miles per hour, and train B left the station at 5 P.M. traveling 50 miles per hour, and you had to determine at what time train A would overtake train B? Problems like this one, and any problems that involve travel, distance, miles per hour, feet per second, planes, trains, or automobiles on the GMAT can be boiled down to one formula:

$$\text{distance} = \text{rate} \times \text{time}$$
$$d = r \times t$$

The problem must give you two of the three variables, so substitute them into the formula and solve. Try this one:

> A plane leaves Chicago at 6 A.M. and is scheduled to arrive in San Francisco, 2,150 miles away, 4 hours later. For the first 2 hours of the trip, the pilot maintains an average speed of 450 miles per hour. If the flight is to arrive as scheduled, what must the plane's average speed be, in miles per hour, for the next 2 hours?
>
> ○ 525
> ○ 550
> ○ 600
> ○ 625
> ○ 650

As soon as you determine that the problem is about travel, jot down your formula, $d = r \times t$, and fill in what you know. The 4-hour trip is divided into 2 parts, the first 2 hours and the last 2 hours, and the question asks you for the average speed of the last 2 hours.

Start with what you know about the first 2 hours: The rate is 450 mph and the time is 2 hours. Using the distance formula, $d = r \times t$, we get $d = 450 \times 2$, or 900 miles. That's the distance traveled in the first 2 hours.

The distance that remains to be covered in the last 2 hours, then, is 1,250 miles (2,150 − 900). Again, plug what you know into the distance formula: $d = r \times t$, so $1,250 = r \times 2$. Solve for r, and you'll get the average speed required for the last 2 hours: 625 miles per hour. The answer is (D).

Work

Work problems are the other type of problems that involve rate on the GMAT. These problems revolve around how quickly a person or machine can complete a job or make a certain number of gadgets, for instance. Although these problems typically involve people or machines working at two different rates for varying lengths of time, it usually all boils down to how much work each can do in one hour. Then, remember to add the rates. Try this one:

> If Anil can finish a job in 4 hours and Gustavo can finish the same job in 6 hours, how long would it take them, working together each at his respective rate, to complete the job?
>
> ○   1 hour, 50 minutes
> ○   2 hours, 10 minutes
> ○   2 hours, 24 minutes
> ○   3 hours, 45 minutes
> ○   4 hours, 30 minutes

For starters, get rid of answer choice (E). If Anil could do the job alone in 4 hours, then with help it should go faster, not slower. This is enough of a reason to be very suspicious of answer choice (D), too.

You should Plug In on a problem like this to make your life easier. Pretend that the job consists of doing something with a specific countable number of separate parts, like drinking 24 sodas. 24 is a good number to pick here, because it's a multiple of both 4 and 6.

Now, let's work the problem:

If Anil can do the whole job in 4 hours, then what is his hourly rate? You can probably do this in your head, but here's the math:

$$\frac{24 \text{ sodas}}{4 \text{ hours}} = \frac{6 \text{ sodas}}{\text{hour}}$$

So Anil's individual hourly rate is 6 sodas per hour.

Now, do the same for Gustavo. He can do the whole job in 6 hours, so he can drink 4 sodas per hour.

But they're working together, so you need to add their individual rates.

$$\frac{6 \text{ sodas} + 4 \text{ sodas}}{\text{hour}} = \frac{10 \text{ sodas}}{\text{hour}}$$

This means that Anil and Gustavo working together can drink 10 sodas in one hour. So how long will it take them to drink 24 sodas?

You can probably see that the answer will be somewhere between 2 and 3 hours, because it would take them exactly 2 hours to drink 20 sodas and exactly three hours to drink 30 sodas. In fact, you could estimate that you're looking for an answer that's a little less than $2\frac{1}{2}$ hours. Rather than jump right into the math, take a look at the answer choices again.

> (A) Wrong. 1 hour 50 minutes is less than 2 hours.
> (B) Might be right.
> (C) Might be right, and seems closer than B.
> (D) Definitely wrong now.
> (E) Already eliminated.

If you were pressed for time on the test, you would pick (C) and move on. If you have time to check your work, finish the math:

$$\frac{24 \text{ sodas}}{10 \text{ sodas}} = 2.4 \text{ hours.}$$

How much is 0.4 hours? Well, it's 0.4 of 60 minutes, and remember that *of* means multiply.

$$0.4 \times 60 = 24$$

So, now we know that it takes them precisely 2 hours and 24 minutes. The answer is (C).

Groups

Remember these?

In a group of 60 children, $\frac{7}{12}$ are girls, $\frac{2}{3}$ are right-handed, and $\frac{2}{5}$ are right-handed girls.
How many of the children are left-handed boys?

- ○ 36
- ○ 24
- ○ 19
- ○ 16
- ○ 9

To tackle a problem like this one, use the formula:

Group 1 + Group 2 + Neither − Both = Total

Group 1 is made up of the children who are girls ($\frac{7}{12}$ of 60, or 35 children) and group 2 is made up of the children who are right-handed ($\frac{2}{3}$ of 60, or 40 children). You know the number of children who are both girls and right-handed ($\frac{2}{5}$ of 60, or 24 children).

You also know the total number of children is 60. Great—you have everything you need to answer the question.

The question asks how many of the children are left-handed boys, so it's really asking how many of the children are neither right-handed nor girls. That's the *Neither*, and that's what you'll solve for. Go ahead and fill in the formula with what you know.

$$\text{Group } 1 + \text{Group } 2 + \text{Neither} - \text{Both} = \text{Total}$$

$$35 + 40 + \text{Neither} - 24 = 60$$

$$75 - 24 + \text{Neither} = 60$$

$$51 + \text{Neither} = 60$$

$$\text{Neither} = 9$$

Nine children are neither right-handed nor girls (they're left-handed boys), and our answer is choice (E).

Average

The **average**, or **arithmetic mean**, of a set of numbers is the sum of the numbers divided by the number of them in the set. The formula for calculating average is $A = \dfrac{T}{N}$, where A = average, T = total (the sum of all the numbers), and N = the number of things you're averaging.

Try this question:

> In a certain month, a pizzeria sold 75 pizzas in the first week, twice as many in the second week as in the first, two-thirds more in the third week than in the first, and three-fifths as many in the fourth week as in the second. What is the average (arithmetic mean) number, per week, of pizzas sold by the pizzeria?
>
> ○ 100
> ○ 105
> ○ 110
> ○ 115
> ○ 120

This problem looks tougher than it is. Start by writing down the formula and then fill in what you know:

$$A = \frac{T}{N}$$

You know N (the number of weeks) is 4, and the question asks you for A, the average. Based on the information given, then, you must be able to determine the total number of pizzas sold. The total is the sum of the number of pizzas sold in each of the 4 weeks. To figure that out, work through the information in the problem in bite-sized pieces.

Week 1 = 75

Week 2 = twice Week 1, or 150

Week 3 = $\frac{2}{3}$ more than Week 1, so $75 + \frac{2}{3}(75) = 75 + 50 = 125$

Week 4 = $\frac{3}{5}$ of Week 2, or $\frac{3}{5}(150 = 90)$

You now know the total number of pizzas sold: 75 + 150 + 125 + 90, or 440. Plug this number into the formula, and solve for the average, A.

$$A = \frac{T}{N}$$

$$A = \frac{440}{4}$$

$$A = 110$$

The answer is choice (C).

On the GMAT, you may also encounter questions related to the mode, median, and range in questions about lists of numbers. The **mode** is the number or term in a list of numbers that occurs most frequently. The **median** is the number in the middle of the list, after you've arranged the numbers in ascending order. The **range** is the difference between the greatest and least values in the list.

So, for the following list of numbers, what are the mode, median, and range?

(25, 13, 36, 25, 40, 25, 13)

First arrange the numbers in ascending order:

(13, 13, 25, 25, 25, 36, 40)

Mode: 25 is the mode, because it is the number that appears most frequently in this list.

Median: The middle number of this seven-number list, 25, is the median. Had there been an even number of terms in the list, the median would have been the average of the two middle numbers. Therefore, the median of a list of numbers might be a number that's not a member of the list itself.

Range: The greatest number in the list is 40, and the least is 13, so the range is their difference, 27.

Ratio

A **ratio** is just another way of representing sizes of parts of a whole. A ratio is always expressed as the relationship of parts to parts (not parts to whole, like a fraction), in most reduced terms. For example, in a bowl of 40 jellybeans, 16 are red and the rest are green. The ratio of red to green jellybeans, then, is 2:3 (16 red jellybeans and 24 green jellybeans, or 16:24, which can be reduced to 2:3).

Probability

Probability is simply the likelihood that a certain event will occur.

Think about rolling a conventional six-sided die, for example. The probability of rolling a 4 is 1 in 6, because there are six possible faces, and only one of them is a 4. Probability is expressed as a fraction in its most reduced form, so the probability of rolling a 4 on a six-sided die is $\frac{1}{6}$.

Try this example:

> In a certain raffle, 500 tickets are sold. Bob purchases 280 of the tickets. What is the probability that one of Bob's tickets will be drawn?

Take the number of possible outcomes that work, 280, and use that as the numerator of a fraction that has 500 as its denominator, and reduce: $\frac{280}{500} = \frac{28}{50} = \frac{14}{25}$.

So, as you can see, Bob has a 14-in-25 chance of winning the lottery. That makes sense—Bob has more than half the tickets, so he has more than a 50 percent shot at winning.

On the GMAT, you might have to figure out the probability of a series of things happening. Remember our six-sided die? The probability of throwing a 4 is $\frac{1}{6}$, but say you have to determine the probability of throwing a 4 on three successive throws. Just multiply the probabilities of each individual throw: $\frac{1}{6} \times \frac{1}{6} \times \frac{1}{6} = \frac{1}{216}$. So there is a 1-in-216 chance of throwing a 4 three times in a row.

You may also be asked to determine the probability when items are not replaced after they are selected. Consider this example:

> There are a total of 10 sandwiches in a picnic basket, 5 of which are ham, 3 of which are roast beef, and 2 of which are turkey. If 3 of the sandwiches are removed at random, what is the probability that all 3 roast beef sandwiches are removed?

○ $\frac{3}{10}$

○ $\frac{2}{45}$

○ $\frac{3}{80}$

○ $\frac{1}{27}$

○ $\frac{1}{120}$

Start by determining the probability that the first sandwich is roast beef; it's $\frac{3}{10}$. Next, start over with what you have left: 9 sandwiches, 2 of which are roast beef. This makes the probability of getting roast beef the second time $\frac{2}{9}$. Now you have 8 sandwiches left, and only

1 is roast beef, so the probability of choosing it is $\frac{1}{8}$. To determine

the probability of getting roast beef all three times, multiply the

individual probabilities together and reduce: $\frac{3}{10} \times \frac{2}{9} \times \frac{1}{8} = \frac{1}{120}$, so

the answer is (E).

FOIL

FOIL (**F**irst, **O**uter, **I**nner, **L**ast) is the process by which you can multiply two binomial terms like this: $(a - 3)(a + 5)$. FOIL reminds you to multiply the first parts of the terms together, then the outer parts, then the inner parts, and finally the last parts of the two terms. It goes like this:

$$(a - 3)(a + 5)$$

First: $a \times a = a^2$

Outer: $a \times 5 = 5a$

Inner: $-3 \times a = -3a$

Last: $-3 \times 5 = -15$

Combine the terms and simplify:

$$a^2 + 5a - 3a - 15 = a^2 + 2a - 15$$

Factoring

Factoring is pretty much just FOIL in reverse. Start by setting up the parentheses and then work backward to figure out the values of the two expressions that must have been multiplied together:

$$x^2 - 7x + 12 = 0$$

What two first terms have been multiplied to get x^2 ? Yes, x and x. Put them in your parentheses as your first terms:

$$(x \quad) (x \quad)$$

Now try to determine which signs go in the middle, based on the sign of the middle and last terms. Your last term, 12, is positive, but your middle term, $-7x$, is negative, so two negative numbers must have been multiplied together in order to get your last term. Put the negative signs in your parentheses.

$$(x - \quad) (x - \quad)$$

Now, to find the last terms, you have to determine what could have been multiplied together to give you 12, but you must keep the Outer/Inner combinations in mind. 12 is the product of 1×12, 2×6, and 3×4. Which set of factors, when added, gives you $7x$? That's right; 3 and 4. Place them in the parentheses and you're done:

$$(x - 3) (x - 4)$$

STEP 6

Reading Comprehension

If you are like many students, Reading Comprehension passages on the GMAT do not sound like something you'd do for fun on a Saturday afternoon. There is no way around the simple fact that most GMAT Reading Comprehension passages are mundane in content and tedious in structure. While it is true that the passages are, for the most part, boring, the good news is that all of the questions can be answered by the information presented in the text. The reading comprehension passages you'll see on the GMAT are 200 to 350 words long. You'll typically see four passages, each of which will be followed by three or four questions. Business, physical science, social science, and biological science are the most commonly discussed topics, but no specialized knowledge of any of these fields is necessary.

The Basic Approach

To successfully answer questions on the GMAT it is important to gain a good understanding of the passage, the question, and the answer choices. By doing so, you will be able to grasp the meaning of the passage, be able to locate information to answer questions quickly and efficiently, and be able to spot incorrect answers. The Basic Approach is a four-step process that will help you feel confident in your abilities to handle any GMAT Reading Comprehension passage.

Here are the steps of the Basic Approach:

Step 1. **Work the Passage.** Read actively and search for the main idea of the passage. Active reading is one of the more important strategies you can master to make yourself a good Reading Comprehension test taker. You can learn to read actively by teaching yourself to ask questions about the passage, the author, and the main point the author is attempting to convey as you read.

Step 2. **Understand the Question Task.** Every question has a subject and a task. Learning to break down the question into these parts will lead to a better understanding of the question and what you need to do to find the information in the passage that will let you complete the next two steps. The subject of the question helps you to find the information you need in the passage. The task will help you to evaluate the information you find about the subject.

Step 3. Find the Information in the Passage That Addresses the Task. Once you have successfully completed Step 2, refer back to the passage to find out what the passage has to say about the subject of the question. Then, link that information to the task of the question. Despite what you may have previously believed about GMAT Reading Comprehension questions, every single answer has to be justified by information from the passage.

Step 4. Use POE to Find the Answer. Process of Elimination (POE) is the best way to attack the answer choices. After completing Steps 1 to 3 of the Basic Approach, you will have a good understanding of what the answer to the question is going to be. However, at any given point, chances are you are reading an incorrect answer choice. After all, four out of the five answers are wrong! Look for signs that the answer choice is incorrect, such as sounding too much like the passage or taking words from the passage out of context. Eliminate answer choices that don't match what you read about the subject in the passage and don't be afraid to simply select the only answer choice that remains if you have good reasons to eliminate the other answer choices.

Question Types

Knowing the question type will allow you to not only quickly identify the subject and task of the question, but also be on the lookout for common wrong answer traps that are often found with certain types of questions.

Common Question Types

There are three categories of questions: *general*, *specific*, and *complex*. Each of those categories has four question types that are commonly tested on the GMAT.

General Questions

The four types of general questions are *main idea, primary purpose, structure,* and *tone.*

Main Idea questions ask you to consider the main claims made by the author. These questions generally ask what the passage is about. The answer to a main idea question summarizes what the author wants you to remember about the passage. A main idea question can be identified by the phrase *main idea* or any reference to an overall claim.

Primary purpose questions may seem a lot like main idea questions, but they differ in one important way. While main idea questions ask what the passage is about, primary purpose questions ask why the author wrote the passage. To answer a primary purpose question you need to figure out why the author wrote the passage. In general, the author wrote the passge to convince you of the passage's main idea! A primary purpose question can be identified by the presence of the phrase *primary purpose* in the question stem.

Structure questions, which are uncommon, ask you to identify the flow of the passage. To answer this question, look through your notes about the passage. The author will follow a structure that you must identify. In many GMAT passages, the author presents an opinion, provides some counterpoints, and then establishes evidence that supports his or her opinion. The task of a structure question is to figure out how the author presented the argument.

Tone questions ask you to evaluate the author's opinion and how strongly the author feels about that opinion. Typically, the question asks about the main topic under discussion in the passage and the author will have expressed an opinion about that topic through the main idea. Start by asking, "Does the author agree or disagree?" If you have found the main idea, deciphering the *tone* of the passage should be a manageable task. These questions are readily identifiable, as the question stem usually includes the word *tone* or *attitude.*

Specific Questions

The four types of specific questions typically found on the GMAT are *retrieval, inference, purpose, and vocabulary in context.*

Retrieval questions, which are very common, are identified by the presence of the words *according to the passage* or a similar phrase that tells you to simply find something stated in the passage. The correct answer is usually just a paraphrase of something the passage said, as retrieval questions ask you to go back to the passage to find some fact or detail.

Inference questions are also very common on the GMAT and often give test takers unaware of the question task the most trouble. These questions usually say something along the lines of *what can be inferred from the passage.* Inference questions will always be about something very specific that is stated in the passage and because of that, are actually very similar to retrieval questions. The answer to an inference question is something that you know to be true based in the information in the passage. Inference questions are easily identified as they usually contain the word *infer, imply,* or *suggest* in the question.

Purpose questions are similar to primary purpose questions in the sense that both ask why the author included certain information in the passage. However, purpose questions ask about something very specific, while primary purpose questions are generally about the bigger picture. These questions can be identified by phrases such as *in order to* and *serves which of the following functions.*

Vocabulary in context questions, which are fairly rare, reference a word or phrase from the passage that the author included to prove a point. The task of these questions is to determine the point or the meaning of the words or phrases indicated in the question stem.

Complex Questions

The four types of complex questions are *evaluation, weaken/strengthen, analogy,* and *application.*

Evaluation questions require test takers to compare or analyze information from the passage. The language used to indicate this type of question varies a lot but an example of this type of question is *Which of the following most accurately summarizes the relationship between nineteenth-century American women and eighteenth-century American women in the highlighted text?* Note here that in print materials, text will not be highlighted. Instead, line reference numbers will be given. But on the actual, computer based test the portions of a question like this will be highlighted. Evaluation questions are one of the least common types of reading questions.

More common than evaluation questions, *weaken/strengthen* questions ask the test taker to weaken or strengthen some claim in the passage. Often, the test taker must consider possible scenarios that could affect the outcome of the claim. Be on the lookout for wrong answers that accomplish the opposite task. For example, answers that weaken are common on strengthen questions. These questions are identified by the presence of the words *weaken* or *strengthen.*

Analogy questions use the answer choices to draw comparisons to information discussed in the passage. The correct answer is the one that has the same characteristics as the information referenced in the passage. Mostly, these questions can be identified by the key phrase *most similar.*

Sometimes questions will ask you to apply information from the passage to a new scenario. These are *application* questions and can be easily spotted when the question stem refers to the answer choices as *scenarios, situations,* or *assertions.*

Common Wrong Answer Choices

Test writers employ common tactics to make wrong answer choices. These tactics are designed to trick the test taker into picking what looks like an attractive answer choice despite the fact that it is incorrect. Having a full understanding of what the passage says about the subject and task of the question will help you to avoid these answer choices, but that is not the only method at your disposal. Being aware of the ways in which incorrect answer choices are commonly created is just as valuable.

The following are the most common ways in which test writers create wrong answers.

Recycled Language and Memory Traps

One of the easiest and most common ways that test writers create a wrong answer choice is by repeating memorable words or phrases from the passage. The correct answers for GMAT Reading Comprehension questions are generally paraphrases of the passage. So the presence of words or phrases that are very reminiscent of the passage is a reason to be skeptical of the answer choice. Any answer choice that evokes a strong memory of the passage should cause suspicion as it could be a Recycled Language or Memory Trap answer.

Extreme Language

Another common way to create wrong answer choices is by using language that is too "powerful" or overt. Common ways to do that are by using words such as *must, always, never, only, best,* and other very strong words; or by answers that use verbs that are really strong, such as *prove* or *fail.* The stronger the claim made in the answer choice, the more likely that answer is to be incorrect. Always compare the language in the answer against the language in the passage to see whether the claim made in the passage is as strong as the claim in the answer choice.

No Such Comparison

Comparison words such as *better, more, reconcile, less, decide,* or *more than* are often used by test writers to make answer choices more appealing by drawing a comparison between two items refer-enced in the passage. However, these items may not have been compared in the passage. If you see comparison words in an answer choice, you should be skeptical.

Reversals

Reversal answer choices seek to confuse the test taker by saying the opposite of either the main idea of the passage or a detail from the passage. However, if you are an active reader who did a good job breaking down the passage to find the main idea, you should be able to spot reversal answer choices.

Emotional Appeals

This answer choice type is fairly rare on the GMAT. Some answer choices may try to appeal to the beliefs of the test taker. For instance, a political passage may contain an answer choice that values one political stance over another even if the passage made no such claim. If you see answer choices like this, be very skeptical and refer back to the passage. You need to pick an answer based on what the passage said rather than your own beliefs about the topic.

Outside Knowledge

Like emotional appeal answer choices, outside knowledge answer choices are fairly rare on the GMAT. Correct answer choices on the GMAT will contain information that is found in the passage. However, these answer choices can be very tempting to the test taker because you may know something that is not mentioned in the passage but that is reflected in an answer choice.

STEP 7

Analytical Writing Assessment

Isn't the GMAT Multiple Choice?

The first scored section of the GMAT is a 30-minute essay called the Analytical Writing Assessment, or AWA. It's GMAC's way of introducing a scored writing component into their multiple-choice test. On what barely passes for a word processor, you'll type your answer to one question in essay form.

The essay task is referred to as Analysis of an Argument. It asks you to support or attack an argument's line of reasoning. Your job is to critique the author's reasoning—that is, the way in which the author structured and supported his or her argument.

How's It Scored?

Your essay will be graded on a scale of 0 (incomprehensible) to 6 (clearly argued and thoughtfully composed). A human reader, who spends about 90 seconds reading your essay, and a computer, which spends considerably less time, each assign a score to your essay. If the two scores differ by more than one point, a second human reader assigns a third score. Otherwise, your two scores are averaged to generate your overall AWA score. This score is reported separately and is not in any way factored into your overall (200 to 800) score or your Integrated Reasoning score.

Why Have the AWA?

Many theories exist to account for the addition of the AWA essays to the GMAT in 1996. Some argue that the writing assessment was added at the request of business schools, who realized that they'd launched generation after generation of CEOs who couldn't write a proper sentence. A more feasible explanation, however, is that since the 1980s b-schools have been inundated with applicants from abroad, all with varying degrees of fluency in English. Business schools wanted a sure-fire method of determining the fluency of their applicants, and a measure against which to compare the essays in the application (to ensure that the applicants authored their own application essays).

Whatever the reason for their existence, it is important to remember the role these essays play in your admission to business school. Most b-schools simply compare the score against the essays in your actual application. If your application essays are scripted in prose that sings off the page, but your AWA score is a 1 or 2, a b-school might consider asking for another writing sample just to verify that you wrote the essays in your application. If English is not your first language, expect b-schools to look more closely at your AWA essays. As long as your essays are at the same level of writing as your application essays, you have nothing to worry about. B-schools know you're writing the AWA under pressure, and that you're nervous about the multiple-choice portion of the test that's still to come; don't worry, they'll take all that into account.

The Environment

Once you've progressed through the tutorial (the untimed portion of the test, in which you're instructed in how to use a mouse, how to scroll, and so on), you'll face the AWA. You'll have 30 minutes to type in your answer for your essay question.

On this portion of the test your word-processing functions are limited to these normal keyboard functions:

Enter:	moves the cursor to the beginning of the next line
Backspace:	removes the character to the left of the cursor
Delete:	removes the character to the right of the cursor
Arrows:	moves the cursor up, down, to the left, or to the right
Page Up:	moves the cursor up one page
Page Down:	moves the cursor down one page
End:	moves the cursor to the end of the line of type
Home:	moves the cursor to the beginning of a line of type

In addition to the keyboard commands above, you'll also see three icons on your screen:

Cut:	Drag your mouse (holding down the mouse button) across all the text you want to move. Then click on the CUT icon. The text you selected will disappear, but it will be stored in the computer's memory.
Paste:	Use the mouse to move your cursor to the place you'd like to insert the text you've cut, and click the PASTE icon. The text you cut will be inserted at that spot.
Undo:	If you cut or pasted text inadvertently, use the undo icon to reverse your most recent action. You can also use UNDO to remove words you've just typed.

These commands may work differently from what you're accustomed to. Keep that in mind as you start to type your essay; do not become flustered or frustrated if you make a mistake.

Overall Strategy

We'll get into specific strategies for the essay in the next few pages, but before you get started, here are some general pointers:

1. **Polish your typing skills.** If you are not in the habit of using a keyboard on a regular basis, take every opportunity between now and test day to practice. We're not suggesting you sign up for a typing class tomorrow, but anything you can do to make the test easier for yourself is a good idea. Although you can probably finish your essays in the allotted time using the old "two-finger" method, the more comfortable you are typing, the less stressed you'll be.

2. **Choose a side, definitively**. You will actually lose points by seeing both strengths and weaknesses in your argument. It doesn't matter which side you choose, but it does matter that you choose one before you start writing.

3. **Plan your attack.** Start your essay by jotting down four or five points in support of the side of the argument you've chosen to defend. Plan to spend at least five minutes on this part of the process. If you brainstorm first, you'll write a better-supported, more organized essay than you will if you jump in and start writing immediately.

4. **Organize your thoughts.** Take the three best points from your brainstorming and transform them into an outline. Decide which point most strongly supports your side and put it first.

5. **Use standard essay format.** Using an introduction, one supporting point per paragraph, and a conclusion, for an overall essay of five to six paragraphs, will help you stay focused as you write, and your essay will be cohesive, organized, and easy to follow. We also recommend you "signpost" along the way, using phrases like *thus* and *primarily* to let your readers know exactly where they are and what to expect next. We'll explore this idea further a little later.

6. **Introduce and conclude first.** Although 30 minutes may seem like plenty of time, your reader will be disappointed if you write a well-supported, intelligent essay, but run out of time before you get to the conclusion. An essay without a conclusion will receive a lower score. You can avoid this by writing the introduction and conclusion first, and using the *cut* and *paste* functions to insert the supporting paragraphs. This may also help you stay organized.

7. **Keep it simple.** Your readers spend about 90 seconds evaluating your writing ability. Complicated sentence construction or 25-cent words, especially if you misuse them, will slow down and distract your readers, and may wear on their patience. You will almost surely be graded down for long-windedness, meandering sentence structure, and wordiness.

8. **Watch your language.** Graders are instructed to ignore minor errors in spelling and grammar. Still, unless you are absolutely sure of the spelling of a word, do not use it. If this means your essay is written exclusively in a one- and two-syllable vocabulary, so be it. You are better off coherently arguing your point with small words used and spelled correctly than with fancy ones that are used incorrectly and spelled wrong.

9. **Proofread.** Watch the clock, and leave yourself a few minutes at the end of your half hour to proofread. No matter how careful a typist you are, you will make mistakes. Give yourself time to catch and correct them so you can present yourself in the best light. If you have trouble proofreading your own writing, and many people do, try reading one word at a time, backwards.

AWA Argument

The Analysis of an Argument essay asks you to critique someone else's point of view. You are not asked to give your opinion on the topic of the argument; rather, your job is to evaluate how well the author supported his or her opinion.

You will be presented with an argument very similar to the ones you'll see in the Verbal section of the test. Each argument will have a conclusion and premises that the author has chosen to support his or her conclusion. You'll need to take apart this argument to determine how well it is reasoned. Whether or not you agree with the author's conclusion is irrelevant.

The strategy you'll use to analyze the author's argument is very similar to the technique you learned to break down an argument in the Critical Reasoning section:

1. Identify the conclusion of the argument, as well as the premises used to support that conclusion.

2. Point out the assumptions that are necessary for the argument's conclusion to be logically drawn.

3. Decide how valid the premises and assumptions are, and how well they support the argument.

4. Identify any places where you find the author's reasoning to be weak and discuss how you would make it stronger.

5. Keep your opinion to yourself. The biggest mistake test takers make is to get involved in the argument. Your job is to critique the author's reasoning, not to make his argument for him.

Let's start with a sample question, and proceed through the building of an Analysis of the Argument essay.

> The state of Vermont, citing the high injury and
> fatality rate in motorcycle accidents, recently
> proposed a law requiring helmets for all
> motorcycle drivers. Although helmets are
> typically instrumental in preventing the type of
> fatalities associated with motorcycle accidents,

the law poses an unnecessary restriction and should not be passed. The state of Vermont already requires all motorcycle operators to be over the age of 18, an age at which they are considered adults, responsible for making decisions about their own welfare. Furthermore, the majority of motorcycle accidents result in fatality only to the operators of the motorcycle, and many of those fatal accidents do not even involve another vehicle, as they occur when the motorcycle collides with a stationary object.

Discuss how well reasoned you find this argument. In your discussion, be sure to analyze the line of reasoning and the use of evidence in the argument. For example, you may need to consider what questionable assumptions underlie the thinking and what alternative explanations or counterexamples might weaken the conclusion. You can also discuss what sort of evidence would strengthen or refute the argument, what changes in the argument would make it more logically sound, and what, if anything, would help you better evaluate its conclusion.

All of the arguments in the AWA section are presented in a standard format. Your response, therefore, should follow a standard essay format. This will make it easier for you to practice writing a good essay, and also make your essay easier to follow.

Let's start by taking this argument apart. First, isolate the author's conclusion and jot it down below.

Conclusion:

Did you say that the author believes the law requiring a helmet for anyone operating a motorcycle should not be passed? Good. Now write down, in your own words, the premises the author uses to support his conclusion. Remember to keep your personal opinions on helmet laws to yourself.

Premise 1:

Premise 2:

Premise 3:

Premise 4:

Here are the author's premises:

- Most motorcycle accidents result in the death of only the driver of the motorcycle.

- Most of the accidents occur when the motorcycle collides with a stationary object.

- Vermont already requires motorcycle operators to be over 18, and 18-year-olds are considered adults, responsible for their own welfare.

- He states that this requirement made the law redundant and unnecessary.

As you were writing down those premises, you probably noticed that the author relied heavily upon certain assumptions, and you may have even thought of some flaws in the logic of the argument. What were they?

Assumptions and/or Flaws:

The author bases his argument on some rather weak reasoning. Here are several of his assumptions:

- The only reason for passing the helmet law is to prevent fatalities of motorcycle drivers.

- There is no other reason for passing the helmet law, such as cutting down expenses to taxpayers.

- Someone who is considered an adult will make responsible decisions about his or her own welfare and the welfare of others.

- Fatalities are the only degree of injury associated with motorcycle accidents.

If you got even half of those, you're in good shape. Let's forge ahead into the writing of the actual essay.

The Format

The *human* essay readers have a very short attention span, and they read as many as 40 AWA essays an hour. They appreciate a formulaic approach, because it makes it easier for them to assess your essay using standard criteria, and to compare it to the other essays they have seen. Your *computer* reader, or e-rater, is even more dogmatic. It has read hundreds of human-scored sample essays on the topic you're writing about, and has developed a series of criteria that all good essays meet.

We said you should write your essay using a standard format, including an introduction, three supporting paragraphs, and a conclusion. Now let's look more closely at what role these three components should perform.

Introduction

Your introduction should quickly recap the author's point and indicate the direction your essay will take. Your job is to identify weaknesses in the author's logical construction. Write your introduction on your noteboard, and then continue.

A good introductory paragraph for our motorcycle argument might read as follows:

> The author states that Vermont's proposed helmet law is redundant and unnecessary and should not be passed. This conclusion is based on faulty reasoning and invalid assumptions, which do not lend sufficient support to the author's thesis.

Body Paragraphs

Choose the three strongest or clearest points from your brain-storming—the points you think weaken the author's argument most effectively. You'll explore these points in your three body paragraphs, each of which should address a different point using two to three sentences.

You can evaluate the believability of the author's assumptions. To do this, you can make suggestions for improving the argument by filling in gaps left by assumptions or by correcting faulty reasoning. Make sure to use details and examples to strengthen your essay. Also, show your reader where you're going by using words like *first*, *additionally*, *furthermore*, and *however*. Try a couple of body paragraphs now, and then take a look at what we've done.

Okay, we think a good body paragraph starts like this:

> *One of the greatest flaws in the argument is that it relies upon the assumption that . . . .*

or

> *Furthermore, the author assumes that [assumption]. He fails to consider the possibility, however, that . . . .*

Conclusion

The concluding paragraph is your opportunity to really drive your point home. It is the last impression your reader will have of your writing, so make it strong. You should begin with clear conclusion words, such as *in conclusion*, *clearly*, or *therefore*. Sum up the criticism you made of the argument and make final recommendations for improvement.

Craft a brief conclusion, and then take a look at what we did.

Here's ours:

> The author's argument against Vermont's proposed helmet law, therefore, is flawed and implausible, as it relies on a series of unsubstantiated premises and fallacious reasoning.

Putting It All Together

As you look over our sample Analysis of an Argument essay to see how closely yours compares, keep in mind that it's more important that your structure and signposting are similar to ours, not that you chose the same assumptions or weak spots in reasoning.

Our Sample Analysis of an Argument

The author says that Vermont's proposed helmet law is redundant and unnecessary and should not be passed. This conclusion is based upon faulty reasoning and invalid assumptions, which do not lend sufficient support to the author's thesis. The author bases his conclusion on facts about the fatality rate in motorcycle accidents and a statement about the ability of those granted motorcycle licenses to make decisions about their own welfare. These premises, however, are neither well reasoned nor sufficient to support the conclusion.

One of the greatest flaws in the argument is that it relies on the assumption that the only reason for passing the helmet law is to prevent fatalities of motorcycle drivers. The author admits that helmets are instrumental in preventing "the type of fatalities associated with motorcycle accidents," yet he overlooks the additional benefits that could result from passing the helmet law. The author does not even discuss the kinds of injuries that can result from motorcycle accidents, such as paralysis and brain damage. Although these injuries are not fatal, they are certainly incapacitating and tragic. Laws such as Vermont's proposed helmet law not only prevent fatalities, but also result in lower incidence of these injuries.

Furthermore, the author states that only those older than 18 years of age can obtain a license to operate a motorcycle, and that 18-year-olds are responsible enough for "making decisions about their own welfare." He fails to consider, however, what kinds of decisions these are. While 18-year-olds may be considered adults legally, that fact alone does not guarantee they will make the rational decision to wear a motorcycle helmet. Additionally, there are already existing laws that override the individual's right to make decisions about his or her own welfare. Seatbelt laws, for example, mandate that every front-seat passenger in a moving vehicle be buckled in. This law is in effect in every state in the United States. So clearly, allowing 18-year-olds to make their own decisions is not sufficient reason to oppose a helmet law.

The strongest argument against the author's point, however, is that preventing fatalities is reason enough to pass a helmet law. The author argues that "the majority of motorcycle accidents result in fatality only to the operator of the motorcycle," citing this as a reason to oppose the law, which is preposterous reasoning. While the operator of a motorcycle may nonchalantly take his life into his own hands, if permitted, by choosing not to wear a helmet, the state cannot permit such choices. The state has an obligation to protect the lives of its citizens, as is evidenced by the illegality of both murder and suicide. Any fatality that could have been prevented by the wearing of a motorcycle helmet is a senseless death; if proponents of the helmet law believe it will circumvent fatalities, that alone is reason enough for its passage.

The author might have strengthened his argument by citing fatality rates before and after the passage of similar laws in states other than Vermont. Had he demonstrated that the helmet law did not result in a lower incidence of fatality, his argument would have been more persuasive. But he did not; he chose to base his thesis on a flimsy assertion about 18-year-olds making their own decisions and the fact that fatalities in motorcycle accidents are limited to the drivers of the motorcycles. The author's argument against the state of Vermont's proposed helmet law, therefore, is flawed and implausible, as it relies on a series of unsubstantiated premises and fallacious reasoning.

Geometry

The good news is that you probably won't encounter much geometry on the GMAT. The bad news is that the GMAT does test a wide base of fundamental geometry knowledge, most of which you learned in tenth grade and may have promptly forgotten. Who uses geometry on a daily basis, besides geometry teachers? To give you a better chance of acing any geometry problem you encounter, we're going to spend this chapter reviewing the main concepts and formulas.

Lines

A **line** is a set of points extending in two directions. When two lines intersect, they form angles.

Angles

The defining characteristic of **angles** is their measurement, or the number of degrees they contain. All angle measurements are relative to a circle, which contains 360°. Half of a circle is a 180° angle, which is also a straight line.

Angles come in three types: **acute** (less than 90°), **right** (equal to 90°), and **obtuse** (greater than 90°).

Parallel Lines

Two lines are considered **parallel** if they are the same distance from one another at all points, and therefore never meet. When parallel lines are intersected by a third line (that isn't perpendicular to them), two angles of different sizes are formed. For now, we'll call them big angles and little angles. All big angles have the same measurement in this situation, and all little angles also have the same measurement. The sum of any big angle and any little angle is 180°, because a big angle plus a little angle forms a line. In the diagram below, l_1 is parallel to l_2, the measure of $\angle x = 145°$, $\angle x = \angle a$, and $\angle a + \angle b = 180°$.

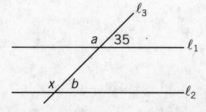

Triangles

A closed, three-sided figure containing three angles is called a **triangle**.

Here are a few facts you'll need to know about triangles:

- The sum of the measurement of all three angles inside a triangle is 180°.
- The largest angle in a triangle is always opposite the longest side.
- The sum of the lengths of any two sides of a triangle is always greater than the length of the third side.

Take a look at the diagram below:

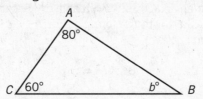

The measurement of angle b is 40°, because the sum of the other two angles is 140°.

$\overline{CB}$ is the longest side, because it is opposite the largest angle.

$\overline{AC} + \overline{AB} > \overline{BC}$; that is, the sum of the lengths of two sides (any two) is greater than the length of the third side.

Triangles are defined by the sizes of their sides. A **scalene triangle** is one in which no two sides are equal, an **isosceles triangle** is one in which two sides are equal, and an **equilateral triangle** is one in which all three sides are equal. A **right triangle** is one that contains a right, or 90°, angle.

The Pythagorean Theorem

On the GMAT, questions about right triangles tend to center on one concept: the Pythagorean theorem.

The **Pythagorean theorem** can be used to determine the length of the sides of a right triangle. This theorem states that, in a right triangle, the square of the length of the longest side, or **hypotenuse**, is equal to the sum of the squares of the other two sides (**legs**). Algebraically, the Pythagorean theorem is written $a^2 + b^2 = c^2$, where c is the hypotenuse.

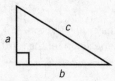

So in the right triangle above, if $a = 3$ and $c = 5$, can you determine the length of b? Start with the formula $a^2 + b^2 = c^2$ and substitute in the values you know.

$$3^2 + b^2 = 5^2$$

$$9 + b^2 = 25$$

$$b^2 = 25 - 9$$

$$b^2 = 16$$

$$b = 4$$

In fact, 3:4:5 is a commonly encountered right triangle on the GMAT, and if you are given two sides, you should automatically know the length of the third.

Now all you have left to learn about triangles are the formulas for perimeter and area. The **perimeter** of a triangle is the sum of the lengths of its sides, so for any triangle with sides a, b, and c, the perimeter is expressed as $a + b + c$.

The **area** of any triangle is expressed by the formula $A = \dfrac{1}{2}bh$, where b is the length of the base and h is the height. The height is simply a perpendicular line drawn from the base of the triangle to the opposite vertex. Any side of the triangle can be considered the base.

Quadrilaterals

Any four-sided figure is a **quadrilateral**. The main quadrilaterals you'll encounter on the GMAT are rectangles and squares.

A **rectangle** is a four-sided figure in which opposite sides are parallel and of equal length, and all angles are 90°. The perimeter of a rectangle is the sum of its sides, and the area is expressed as $A = lw$, where l is the length of one side of the rectangle and w is the length of a side that is perpendicular to the length.

A **square** has four equal sides and four right angles. If s represents a side, then the perimeter of a square is $4s$ and its area is s^2.

Circles

A **circle** is a set of points in a plane that are equidistant from a given point. A circle contains 360°. A line drawn from the center of the circle to any point on the circle is called its **radius**. All radii are of equal length. A line that connects two points on the circumference of a circle and intersects the center of the circle is called a **diameter**. An **arc** is a portion of the circumference of the circle.

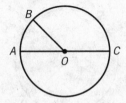

In the circle above, $\overline{OB}$ is a radius, $\overline{AC}$ is a diameter, and AB is an arc.

Two important formulas to memorize for circles are those for the **circumference** (the distance around the circle) and the area. Both formulas contain the constant π, or *pi*. You don't need to know the numerical value of π, just recognize that it is a little more than 3.

Circumference: $C = 2\pi r$ (*r* is the length of a **radius**)

Area: $A = \pi r^2$

So, in our circle above, if the radius $r = 3$, let's find the circumference and area.

Circumference:

$$C = 2\pi r$$

$$C = 2\pi(3)$$

$$C = 6\pi$$

Area:

$$A = \pi r^2$$

$$A = \pi(3)^2$$

$$A = 9\pi$$

You may see questions that ask about only a portion of a circle. For example, you may need to find the area of the shaded portion of the figure below, in which the measure of $\angle AOB = 90°$.

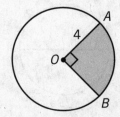

Start by looking at the angle at the center of the circle, and determine what fractional part of the circle it represents. The angle measures 90°, which is $\frac{1}{4}$ of 360°. So the shaded region is $\frac{1}{4}$ of the area of the circle. Since we know that the radius is 4, we know the area of the entire circle is 16π. $\frac{1}{4}$ of 16π is 4π, and that's the area of the shaded region.

Coordinate Geometry

Coordinate geometry, or **Cartesian geometry,** is based on a grid formed by two number lines intersecting to form right angles. The horizontal line is called the **x-axis**, and the vertical line is called the **y-axis**. Their intersection is called the **origin**. The diagram below represents the grid used for coordinate geometry.

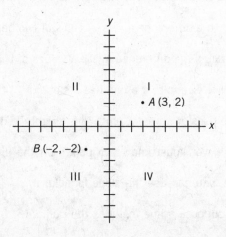

Locations on the grid are called **points** or **coordinate pairs**, and are defined by their distance from the origin, along the x- and y-axes. So point A on our diagram is (3, 2), because the x-coordinate (the first one in the pair) is 3 units to the right of 0, and the y-coordinate (the second one) is 2 units up from 0.

The quarters of a grid are called **quadrants**. They are numbered counterclockwise, beginning with the upper right quadrant. So Quadrant I contains all positive *x* and *y* coordinate points (+*x*, +*y*), Quadrant II contains all negative *x* and positive *y* coordinate points (–*x*, +*y*). Point *B* on our diagram is located in Quadrant III, which contains all negative *x*- and *y*-coordinate points, and Quadrant IV contains all positive *x*-coordinate and negative *y*-coordinate points.

Every line in the coordinate grid can be expressed by the equation *y* = *mx* + *b*, which is commonly called the **slope intercept** equation for a line. Let's review what each variable stands for in this formula:

- *y* is the *y*-coordinate of a point.

- *x* is the *x*-coordinate of the same point.

- *b* is the *y*-intercept, or the *y*-coordinate of the point at which the line crosses the *y*-axis (when *x* is equal to zero).

- *m* is the slope of the line.

The **slope** of a line indicates its steepness as a ratio of rise over run. The **rise** is the difference in the *y*-values of two points on a line ($y_1 - y_2$). The **run** is the difference in the *x*-values of two points on a line ($x_1 - x_2$). For example, if a line has a slope of $\frac{1}{2}$, then for every 1 unit the line rises, it moves 2 units to the right. To determine the slope of a line, you must know two points on the line. To calculate the slope, you can use the **slope formula:** $m = \dfrac{\text{rise}}{\text{run}} = \dfrac{y_1 - y_2}{x_1 - x_2}$. For example, suppose a line includes the points (6, 0) and (2, 3).

Here's how to find the slope of that line:

$$\frac{y_1 - y_2}{x_1 - x_2} = \frac{0 - 3}{6 - 2} = -\frac{3}{4}$$

Now you know that for every 4 units the line runs across, it rises up or down by 3. The (–) tells us that the line goes down from left to right. Lines with positive slopes go up from left to right.

Okay, so back to the line, $y = mx + b$. If you know one point on the line and you know the slope, you can determine the y-intercept and plot the line on the coordinate grid. Suppose that you know that the point (2, 3) is on a line that has a slope of 5. To find the y-intercept, start by substituting in the slope for m in the equation $y = mx + b$. Then, fill in the point you know for x and y and solve for b:

$$y = 5x + b$$

$$3 = (5)(2) + b$$

$$3 = 10 + b$$

$$b = -7$$

So, the y-intercept of the line with slope 5 that contains the point (2, 3) is –7.

Statistics and Spare Parts

Only a few topics remain for you to learn. They show up fairly infrequently on the GMAT, but you should still be prepared to face them. These topics include some basic statistics (very basic) and a hodgepodge of other pet topics of GMAC. You're most likely to see questions on the topics covered in this chapter if you are scoring above 600 overall.

Counting and Factorials

At the end of the Formulas chapter, we discussed probability, which deals with the likelihood of a certain event occurring. But GMAC may ask you about the number of ways that you can combine events or things—for example, the number of ways 3 violinists, 2 cellists, and 4 bassists can be combined to form a trio of musicians. These types of manipulations are called combinations or permutations, depending on whether their order matters. We'll walk you through both, but first we need to teach you about factorials.

A **factorial** looks like this: $x!$. The exclamation point means that you multiply the number by every positive integer less than the number. Try it with 5:

$$5! = 5 \times 4 \times 3 \times 2 \times 1 = 120$$

You get the picture. Most of the time, you'll reduce the factorial before you multiply it, so it won't get so messy that you'll need a calculator. Factorials are used to express the number of possibilities in problems dealing with combinations and permutations.

Combinations

Let's start with **combinations**, that is, counting the number of different ways a group of things can be combined.

A dance team with 5 members will perform, 2 dancers at a time, until all the possible combinations of dancers have performed. If each combination dances for 5 minutes, and there are no breaks or interruptions, what is the total running time of the performance?

- ○   80 minutes
- ○   75 minutes
- ○   60 minutes
- ○   50 minutes
- ○   45 minutes

This is not as tough as it sounds. Here's the formula you need (memorize it):

$$C = \frac{n!}{r!(n-r)!}$$

In this formula, n is the total number of things in the group and r is the number of things you're selecting. So in the problem about the dancers, $n = 5$ and $r = 2$.

The number of combinations of dancers, then, is

$$C = \frac{n!}{r!(n-r)!}$$

$$C = \frac{n!}{2!(5-2)!}$$

$$C = \frac{5!}{2!(3)!}$$

At this point, write out the factorials so you can start reducing:

$$C = \frac{5 \times 4 \times 3 \times 2 \times 1}{2 \times 1(3 \times 2 \times 1)}$$

Notice that 3 × 2 × 1 is on both the top and bottom, so you can reduce that part to 1. You're left with $C = \dfrac{5 \times 4}{2 \times 1}$, which reduces to $C = \dfrac{20}{2}$, or 10. So there are 10 combinations of dancers. If each performs for 5 minutes, the total performance time is 50 minutes, and the answer is (D).

Permutations

In the preceding problem, the order in which the dancers perform doesn't matter; you simply count the number of combinations. But when order does matter, the question is talking about a **permutation**.

> Five runners compete in a race for which first, second, and third place prizes are awarded. In how many different ways could these prizes be awarded to these runners?
>
> ○   5
> ○   20
> ○   60
> ○   90
> ○   120

To solve a permutation problem, use this formula (memorize this one too):

$$P = \frac{n!}{(n-r)!}$$

In this formula, n is the total number in the group you're drawing from, and r is the number of things you're arranging. So, in the problem above, $n = 5$ and $r = 3$.

$$P = \frac{n!}{(n-r)!}$$

$$P = \frac{5!}{(5-3)!}$$

$$P = \frac{5!}{2!}$$

$$P = \frac{5 \times 4 \times 3 \times 2 \times 1}{2 \times 1}$$

Remember to reduce before you proceed. You're left with $P = 5 \times 4 \times 3$, or 60. There are 60 possible arrangements of contestants, so the answer is choice (C).

Functions

GMAC may also try to confuse you with a question that looks like this:

If $p \Delta q = \dfrac{p(p-q)}{q^2}$, then what is the value of $4 \Delta 5$?

But don't worry. The little triangle is not some obscure symbol whose meaning you've forgotten. It's simply GMAC's way of making a straightforward problem more complicated. Ignore the funky symbol and follow the directions you're given. Everywhere you see a p in the first equation, put a 4, and everywhere you see a q, replace it with 5. Then solve.

$$p \Delta q = \frac{p(p-q)}{q^2}$$

$$4 \Delta 5 = \frac{4(4-5)}{5^2}$$

$$= \frac{4(-1)}{25}, \text{ or } -\frac{4}{25}$$

Easy enough, right?

Simultaneous Equations

Two or more equations that contain the same set of variables are called **simultaneous equations**. Here's the cardinal rule of simultaneous equations: As long as you have the same number of distinct equations as you have variables, you can solve for the variables. Therefore, solving for two variables requires two distinct equations, three variables require three distinct equations, and so on.

Simultaneous equations appear most often in data sufficiency problems, and they look like this:

> What is the value of y ?
> (1) $6x + 10y = 42$
> (2) $5x - 3y = 1$

or

> How many girls are in the chess club?
> (1)   The chess club has a total of 50 members.
> (2)   Twice the number of boys in the chess club is equal to three times the number of girls in the chess club.

You do not need to solve the equations. As long as you determine that you have two distinct equations and two of the same variables in each equation, you know that you need both statements together, and your answer is (C). Both statements together are sufficient to answer the question asked, but neither statement alone is sufficient. A final note: This works only with linear equations, that is, equations with no exponents. If your simultaneous equations have exponents, you'll have to go ahead and work through them.

Combining Ranges for Inequalities

First, let's review the symbols:

> means *greater than*

≥ means *greater than or equal to*

For instance, 5 > 3 reads as 5 *is greater than* 3.

< means *less than*

≤ means *less than or equal to*

So $x \leq y$ reads x is less than or equal to y.

≠ means *is not equal to.*

So $x \neq 0$ means x *is not equal to 0.*

When you're working within inequalities, you can manipulate and solve them just as you do equations, with one important exception. If you multiply or divide both sides by a negative number, you have to reverse the inequality symbol.

Inequalities on the GMAT tend to present you with a range of values for your variables. Here's an example:

> If $-6 \leq a \leq 12$ and $3 \leq b \leq 10$, which of the following represents the possible values of ab?
>
> ○ $-60 \leq ab \leq 120$
>
> ○ $-60 \leq ab \leq -18$
>
> ○ $-18 \leq ab \leq 36$
>
> ○ $-18 \leq ab \leq 120$
>
> ○ $36 \leq ab \leq 120$

To solve, try all four combinations of the endpoints of the ranges to see which gives you greatest and the least possible values for the required operation. The least ab can equal is (-6×10) or -60, and the greatest ab can equal is (12×10) or 120, so the answer is $-60 \leq ab \leq 120$, or (A).

Interest

You've probably patronized banks for most of your life, but you may never have had to calculate interest on an account. Rest assured, it isn't as difficult as it might sound. There are two types of interest: simple and compound. We'll start with simple interest, because it's, well, more simple.

Take a look at the problem below:

> If Andrew deposits $800 in a savings account that pays 3% interest annually, how much money will be in the account after one year?
>
> ○ $803
> ○ $816
> ○ $824
> ○ $832
> ○ $840

Simple interest is just a thinly disguised percentage problem, so translate:

What is 3% of $800?

$$x = \frac{3}{100} \times 800$$

$$x = 3 \times 8, \text{ or } 24$$

So Andrew's account gained $24 in one year, and the total in his savings account is now $824. The answer is choice (C).

Compound interest comes up so rarely that you'll be fine if you ballpark on problems dealing with it. In reality, compound interest usually yields just a little more than simple interest. This means that you can usually just compute the simple interest for the problem, and choose the next highest answer. Be careful, though—the simple interest will almost always be an answer choice, and it's a trap.

Standard Deviation

It should not be surprising to you that GMAC asks questions about **bell curves**. After all, the bell curve is their entire reason for being. You may have encountered bell curves in college—test grades in large classes are often given according to a bell curve.

Imagine that 100 students have taken a test. All of the students' grades are plotted in relation to the average, or mean, score on the test. If their tests are graded according to a bell curve, the number of A's is equal to the number of F's, the number of B's is equal to the number of D's, and a majority of the students get C's. Plotted on the curve, the grades would look like this:

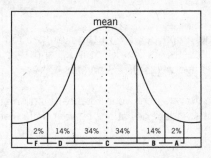

Of the 100 students, 2% gets A's, and 2% gets F's, 14% gets B's and D's, and 68% of the class receives C's. A graph of this type is considered a **normal distribution** and that's the only kind of distribution you'll see. This distribution represents the percentages for all normal bell curves. The percentages above and below the mean, 34, 14, and 2, are always the same. They represent a standard deviation from the mean. So the group of 34% above and the group of 34% below the mean is the first deviation, the two groups of 14% are the second deviation, and the two groups of 2% are the third deviation. Together, all the deviations represent 100% of the group. Deviations will be given as a number, and that number will tell you how far apart the values associated with the deviations are. Sketch out the graph, find the average, and add the deviation to find the values of each group.

Don't worry too much about what all this means. Just know how a bell curve works, and memorize the percentages (34, 14, and 2), and you'll be fine. Try this question for practice:

> The total weight of a group of 100 fish is 2,800 pounds. If the weight of these fish has a normal distribution and the standard deviation equals 4 pounds, approximately how many of the fish weigh more than 32 pounds?
>
> ○   14
> ○   16
> ○   34
> ○   48
> ○   50

To figure out the graph, start with the average. You know that the total weight of the fish is 2,800 pounds, and that there are 100 fish, so their average weight is 28 pounds.

Now jot down that average on your noteboard, and make seven markings to represent standard deviations on your bell curve, like this:

Label the middle one with your average, and fill in the percentages for each deviation.

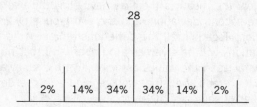

Now label each deviation. To do this, add the number you were given as the deviation to the number you found for your average. Your average is 28 and the deviation is 4 pounds, so the first deviation above the mean is 32 pounds, and the first deviation below the mean is 24 pounds.

Here's a completed bell curve for this problem:

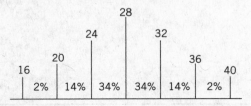

The question asks how many of the fish weigh more than 32 pounds. That would be all of the fish above the first deviation, and that's 16% of the fish (14% in the second deviation and 2% in the third). Since 16% of 100 fish is 16 fish, the answer is choice (B).

The Final Step

The Night Before

You're bound to be anxious the night before the GMAT. That's normal, but try not to freak out or stay up all night cramming. Here are a few things we recommend.

Getting It All Together

The night before, gather together everything you'll need on test day and put it in a sealed plastic bag or a shopping bag. Put that bag in a place where you won't forget it.

Here's a list of things you'll need:

- **Your admissions ticket or confirmation numbers**
- **Directions to the test center and the center's phone number**
- **A light snack, like peanut butter crackers or an apple (steer clear of sugary foods)**
- **Some practice problems to warm up your brain**

Cram the Smart Way

We don't recommend you study much the night before the test. Instead, get a massage, have a nice dinner out, or catch a light movie. If you feel that you must study, use your time wisely. To avoid becoming frustrated, review subject areas in which you're fairly confident. Don't revisit a problem that you've looked at six times and still don't understand—it will only raise your anxiety level. Instead, read through any notes you've made or review the techniques you've learned.

Don't Go Changing

Last of all, don't make any big changes in your life, especially the night before the test. If you normally go to bed at 10, go to bed at 10. If you usually eat a balanced breakfast or run a few miles in the morning, do so on test day. There's no reason to disrupt your normal routine—you'll just feel disoriented and perform less than your best.

The Big Day

At the Testing Center

Be sure to arrive at the testing center with time to spare. It's better to sit around in a lobby for 10 minutes than it is to rush in at the last minute, flustered and distracted. Use any extra time to work through some practice problems so your brain is warmed up when the test starts. When you arrive at the testing center, the proctor will ask you to sign in, you'll put your valuables in a locker, and the proctor will take a digital picture of you.

The proctor will give you a set of noteboards and two markers for writing on the noteboards. Then, you'll be escorted to your computer terminal. The proctor will log you in so that you can start your test. Go ahead and get comfortable.

Tutorial

Your testing experience will start with an onscreen tutorial, during which you'll be instructed on how to use a mouse, how to scroll, and how to perform other computer skills that you probably learned the first day you used a PC.

When you tell the computer you've had enough of the tutorial, your test will begin. Remember that you'll see the AWA essay first.

Focus and Move On

This is the real thing, so stay focused. During the test, there should be only two things on your mind: the problem in front of you and the time on the clock.

If you think you made a mistake on a problem you just finished, forget about it. There's nothing you can do about a problem once you've clicked ANSWER CONFIRM. Don't try to guess how well you're doing by assessing the difficulty of the problem in front of you— most people would guess incorrectly anyway. And even if you think you messed up the first section, give the second section everything you've got—you could be totally wrong about your performance.

Getting Your Score

When you've completed your last multiple-choice section, the computer may ask you to complete a marketing questionnaire. Read the instructions closely—you should know what you're getting into if you choose to proceed, and what you're missing (nothing) if you choose to skip it.

Finally, it's time to see your scores. The computer will show you your scores for the Integrated Reasoning, Quantitative, and Verbal sections and your overall (200–800) score. You have two minutes to decide whether to keep or cancel your scores.

To get the most out of the preview feature, know what scores you are willing to accept before you walk into the test. After all, two minutes isn't a very long time to weigh all the alternatives!

If you do wind up canceling your scores, you have 60 days to reinstate them. However, reinstating your scores costs an additional $100.

If you decide to keep your scores, the proctor will give you a printout of your scores on your way out. This report is unofficial because it doesn't include your essay score. You'll get your official score report in about two weeks.

PART III
Drills

Verbal Drills

Sentence Correction

1. <u>Unlike the United States, where the head of state is chosen in a popular election separate from that which determines the majority party of the legislative branch, the Prime Minister of India</u> is elected by the members of the majority party of Parliament.

    ○ Unlike the United States, where the head of state is chosen in a popular election separate from that which determines the majority party of the legislative branch, the Prime Minister of India

    ○ Unlike the United States, in which the head of state is chosen in a popular election separate from that which determines the majority party of the legislative branch, the Prime Minister of India

    ○ Unlike that of the United States, where a popular election separate from that which determines the majority party of the legislative branch chooses the head of state, India has a Prime Minister that

    ○ In comparison with the United States, where a popular election separate from that which determines the majority party of the legislative branch chooses the head of state, the Prime Minister of India

    ○ In the United States, the head of state is chosen in a popular election separate from that which determines the majority party of the legislative branch, but in India the Prime Minister

2. While five years ago, only 10 percent of
   women said they kept a handgun for home
   security, today that figure is 35 percent,
   making handguns the most popular type of
   home security for women <u>as well as men</u>.

   ○   as well as men
   ○   as well as for men
   ○   and men too
   ○   and men as well
   ○   and also men

3. Even though the Mt. Everest team began the
   expedition with more provisions than <u>they had
   in any previous year</u>, its food lasted through
   only the first twelve days of the climb.

   ○   they had in any previous year
   ○   their previous years had had
   ○   they had for any previous year
   ○   in their previous years
   ○   it had in any previous year

4. <u>With their similar price ranges and menus, "theme" restaurants located in shopping malls often succeed despite the fact that they are clustered next to one another; one reason is suggested by the behavior of their customers, who would rather eat in proximity to the area in which they are shopping than leave the area to eat, even if this means choosing from limited options.</u>

○   With their similar price ranges and menus, "theme" restaurants located in shopping malls often succeed despite the fact that they are clustered next to one another; one reason is suggested by the behavior of their customers, who would rather eat in proximity to the area in which they are shopping than leave the area to eat, even if this means choosing from limited options.

○   If clustered next to each other in shopping malls, one reason that "theme" restaurants with similar price ranges and menus succeed is suggested by the behavior of their customers, who would rather eat in the area in which they are shopping than leave the area to eat, even if this means choosing from limited options.

○   If clustered next to each other in shopping malls, one reason that "theme" restaurants with similar price ranges and menus succeed is suggested by their customers, who would rather eat in proximity to the area in which they are shopping even if this means choosing from limited options than those who would rather leave the area to eat.

○ The fact that there are customers who would rather eat in the area in which they are shopping even if this means choosing from limited options than leave the area to eat is suggestive of one reason, if clustered next to one another in shopping malls, "theme" restaurants with similar price ranges and menus can succeed.

○ The fact that there are customers who would rather eat in the area in which they are shopping than leave the area to eat suggests one reason "theme" restaurants with similar price ranges and menus located in shopping malls can succeed despite being clustered next to one another.

5. Many economic analysts believe that a substantial increase in the number of nonprofessionals using online trading services should lead to raising the overall volume of the market, as well as lowering fears about investing, and a surge in public confidence in the economy.

○ raising the overall volume of the market, as well as lowering fears about investing

○ a raising of the overall volume of the market, a lowering of fears about investing

○ a raising of the overall volume of the market, along with lowering fears about investing

○ the overall volume of the market being raised, along with fears about investing being lowered

○ the overall volume of the market raising, and fears about investing lowering

6. In the latter years of the Great Depression, colleagues of Franklin <u>Roosevelt's argued that his proposed Social Security Act has</u> a good chance of succeeding due to its strong bipartisan support, sound fiscal plan, and widespread electoral approval.

- ○ Roosevelt's argued that his proposed Social Security Act has
- ○ Roosevelt's argued that his proposed Social Security Act had
- ○ Roosevelt's have argued that his proposed Social Security Act had
- ○ Roosevelt argued that his proposed Social Security Act had
- ○ Roosevelt had argued that his proposed Social Security Act has

7. <u>From 1995 to 1998 the average daily retail sales of women's apparel increased between 12 and 16 percent annually.</u>

- ○ From 1995 to 1998 the average daily retail sales of women's apparel increased between 12 and 16 percent annually.
- ○ Twelve to sixteen percent is the annual increase in the average daily retail sales of women's apparel in the years 1995 to 1998.
- ○ The average daily retail sales of women's apparel have increased annually 12 and 16 percent in the years 1995 to 1998.
- ○ Annually an increase from 12 to 16 percent has occurred between 1995 and 1998 in the average daily retail sales of women's apparel.
- ○ Occurring from 1995 to 1998 was an annual increase of 12 to 16 percent in the average daily retail sales of women's apparel.

8. An uncommon method of home building relies on the construction of extremely thick walls to reduce the energy needs due to heating and cooling; the resulting building, with <u>internal spaces that maintain a constant temperature although the outside air that flows through them varies in temperature, are known as "earth ships."</u>

○ internal spaces that maintain a constant temperature although the outside air that flows through them varies in temperature, are known as "earth ships."

○ internal spaces that maintain a constant temperature although they are supplied by varying temperatures of outside air, are known as "earth ships."

○ internal spaces that maintain a constant temperature although the outside air that flows through them varies in temperature, is known as an "earth ship."

○ constant temperature internal spaces although the outside air that flows through them varies in temperature, are known as "earth ships."

○ internal spaces that maintain a constant temperature although they are supplied by varying temperatures of outside air, is known as an "earth ship."

9. In most major metropolitan areas, the number of hate crimes per capita is significantly lower in neighborhoods in which the population is racially mixed, <u>that is, no more than one-third of the area's inhabitants belong to the same ethnic group; it is theorized that a person is less likely to commit a hate crime against someone who he regards as a neighbor.</u>

○ that is, no more than one-third of the area's inhabitants belong to the same ethnic group; it is theorized that a person is less likely to commit a hate crime against someone who he regards as a neighbor

○ that is, no more than one-third of the area's inhabitants belong to the same ethnic group; it is theorized that a person is less likely to commit a hate crime against someone whom he regards as a neighbor

○ that is, no more than one-third of the area's inhabitants belongs to the same ethnic group; it is theorized that a person is less likely to commit a hate crime against someone whom he regards as a neighbor

○ that is, no more than one-third of the area's inhabitants belongs to the same ethnic group; it is theorized that a person is less likely to commit a hate crime against someone who he regards as a neighbor

○ that is, no more than one-third of the area's inhabitants belongs to the same ethnic group; it is theorized that a person is less likely to commit a hate crime against someone whom he regards to be a neighbor

10. <u>Each of Henry VIII's six wives—excluding Jane Seymour, who died in childbirth, and Katherine Parr, who outlived him—were either divorced by Henry or executed by the state.</u>

○ Each of Henry VIII's six wives—excluding Jane Seymour, who died in childbirth, and Katherine Parr, who outlived him—were either divorced by Henry or executed by the state.

○ Excluding Jane Seymour, who died in childbirth, and Katherine Parr, who outlived him, each of Henry VIII's six wives were either divorced by Henry or executed by the state.

○ With the exception of Jane Seymour, who died in childbirth, and Katherine Parr, who outlived him, every one of Henry VIII's six wives were either divorced by Henry or executed by the state.

○ Each of Henry VIII's six wives—excluding Jane Seymour, who died in childbirth, and Katherine Parr, who outlived him—was either divorced by Henry or executed by the state.

○ Divorced by Henry VIII or executed by the state were each of Henry VIII's six wives, excluding Jane Seymour, who died in childbirth, and Katherine Parr, who outlived him.

Arguments

1. A researcher concluded her report on a study testing a new antihypertension drug by saying, "Patients who used the new drug have experienced no significant side effects." The editor of the medical journal to which she submitted the report suggested that she change the conclusion to "Patients who used the new drug appear thus far to have experienced no significant side effects."

   Which of the following, if true, provides the best logical justification for the editor's suggestion that the researcher's conclusion be altered?

   ○ Some patients who took the new antihypertension drug experienced a mild increase in nausea, a side effect easily averted by taking the medication with food.

   ○ The new antihypertension drug could have caused side effects, the visible signs of which have not yet appeared in the patients who participated in the study.

   ○ The researcher's report does not sufficiently compare the effects of the antihypertension drug with those of other, established antihypertension drugs.

   ○ The majority of Americans have blood pressure far enough outside the normal range to be considered at least mildly hypertensive.

   ○ The severity of side effects from antihypertension drugs varies from patient to patient.

2. The World Bank has developed a computer program that assesses the authenticity of world currency suspected of being counterfeit. The program contains extensive profiles of the printing techniques and components of currencies of all major nations; such profiles include chemical composition of paper, density of ink, and details in the printing plates that are invisible to the naked eye. Counterfeiters, including the best counterfeiters known from history, cannot hope to reproduce all facets of a particular nation's currency.

Which of the following can be logically concluded from the passage above?

○ The staff resources required to prepare currency for analysis by the program make use of the program prohibitively expensive.

○ Consumer banks will soon purchase the right to use the program on their own computers.

○ The program cannot fail to identify as inauthentic counterfeit currency that has previously escaped detection.

○ The authentication program has taken a number of years to develop.

○ In numerous cases, authentic currency is not recognized as authentic by the program.

3. **Director of Foreign Language School:** We should stop giving our students the *La Langue Facile* tape series and begin to distribute the *Les Bons Mots* series instead.

Assistant Director: Why?

Director: Because it takes 31 percent more time for teachers to prepare lessons using the *La Langue Facile* tape series than it takes for teachers to prepare lessons using the *Les Bons Mots* tape series. This time would be better spent working directly with students.

Assistant Director: That is not a sufficient reason to change instructional tapes. We can simply hire teachers who already have planned lessons based on the *La Langue Facile* tape series.

Which of the following, if true, most seriously undermines the assistant director's objection to the argument made by the director?

○ All teachers in the school district are currently required to attend classes to learn how to adapt the *La Langue Facile* tapes to new educational standards.

○ Once teachers have made lesson plans, they are more willing to move from their current positions to positions with new language schools.

○ Teachers with established lesson plans hired by foreign language schools are required to put in additional hours in administrative support, hours equal to the time they would have spent in making lesson plans.

○ The average improvement in scores on tests of fluency in the director's school is below the average improvement in standardized test scores in otherwise comparable schools.

○ The supplemental course materials required for use with the *Les Bons Mots* tape series require teachers to invest a great deal of time in logistical arrangements, such as arranging for videocassette recorders and photocopying quizzes.

4.   An automobile manufacturer's engineering department developed a new model of its best-selling sedan that lacked certain safety features present in the earlier model, which was still being produced. During the first year of production of the new model, while both models were being sold, the newer model of the sedan sold much better than the older model. The CEO of the automobile company concluded that safety features were not important in consumers' decisions to purchase the sedan.

Which of the following, if true, would most seriously weaken the CEO's conclusion?

○ The automobile company sells cars both for inclusion in corporate fleets and for individual use.

○ Many customers consider the new sedan safe because of certain features in its steering mechanism and body style.

○ Many of those who purchased the new sedan also own another car manufactured by the same automobile company.

○ The new sedan has sold to more customers in the 18-to-25 age bracket.

○ There was no significant difference in price between the newer sedan and the older model.

5. A new company can offer stocks in an initial public offering (IPO) before the company has proven itself capable of generating long-term profits for its stockholders. Historically, if a company has seemed likely to generate profits, the stock price in the IPO has risen; if the company seemed less likely to generate profits, the stock price in the IPO has fallen. Today business analysts announced that the Tenon Corporation has turned a profit in the financial quarter just completed. Therefore, stock prices for the Tenon Corporation's IPO, which is planned for next week, will rise.

The author's conclusion about Tenon Corporation is based on faulty reasoning because it

○ depends on the assumption that what has been true in the past will hold true in the future

○ relies on a line of reasoning that is circular

○ confuses cause with effect

○ overlooks cases in which the counterexample is true

○ rests on a faulty comparison

6. A company that disposes of industrial waste employs dozens of people in jobs that are considered quite hazardous. The company obeys federal regulations governing workplace safety, and to comply with new regulations instituted to avoid recently discovered risks from airborne particulate matter, company engineers were required to install extremely expensive air-filtering equipment. However, despite the expense of the air-filtering equipment, the company's operating costs for the quarter were considerably lower than normal.

Which of the following, if true, most helps to resolve the apparent paradox?

○ More than half the company's expenditures to maintain worker safety go to pay for protective garments, yet only a small percentage of such expenditures go to pay for nose and mouth filters.

○ Expensive shutdowns to prevent contamination that were periodically required prior to the installation of the air-filtering equipment are no longer necessary.

○ The company's costs of labor, which make up a large fraction of operating costs, increased during the same period.

○ When the air-filtering equipment was installed in the waste disposal facility, the company took the opportunity to upgrade the temperature control equipment.

○ The majority of the company's employees work in the areas of the plant in which the air-filtering equipment was installed.

7. The diamond mines of Extopia produced so many diamonds that the market was overwhelmed; consumption did not keep pace with production. As a result, diamond prices fell. The government of Extopia attempted to support diamond prices through a subsidy scheme: Diamond producers who voluntarily limited the number of diamonds they produced were compensated directly by the government up to a specified maximum payment.

The program instituted by the government of Extopia, if successful, will not result in a net cost increase to the government. Which of the following, if true, is the best basis for an explanation of how this could be true?

○ Depressed diamond prices meant operating losses for diamond producers, decreasing the income of diamond producers, and thus decreasing the taxes paid to the government by diamond producers.

○ Diamond production in countries other than Extopia declined in the same year Extopia's government instituted the compensatory scheme.

○ In the first quarter after Extopia's government instituted the compensatory scheme, diamond production declined 8 percent.

○ Because the government specified a maximum subsidy payment per diamond producer, those producers with numerous mines in operation received less support per mine than those producers with fewer mines in operation.

○ Diamond producers desiring to qualify for the compensatory scheme could not continue to produce diamonds and simply withhold them from the market.

8. Pharmaceutical companies typically charge slightly inflated prices for drugs that have a large customer base and are heavily prescribed by doctors, in order to balance the losses such companies experience from producing "orphan" drugs—drugs that are used by so few patients that they can never be profitable. New federal regulations require pharmaceutical companies to limit the price they charge for any drug to cost plus a predetermined percentage profit.

If the statements above are true, which of the following must also be true?

○ New pharmaceutical technology has made advances possible; the drugs produced by such technology, however, are too expensive for all but the wealthiest patients.

○ If pharmaceutical companies do not find another source of income to balance the losses they experience in producing orphan drugs, such companies will no longer be able to produce those drugs without compromising overall profits.

○ Some patients already request generic pharmaceuticals, when they are available, because they are typically less expensive than name-brand pharmaceuticals.

○ If pharmaceutical companies reduce the costs of producing most drugs, they will be able to earn more profits despite the new law, and thus will be able to balance the losses they experience from the production of orphan drugs.

○ Even though charitable organizations that fund research into the rare diseases treated by orphan drugs provide some donations to offset the costs of the drugs, such donations are declining.

9. Gas leaks are a danger for households in which certain standards of safety are not maintained. So that householders are able to detect such hazards before they become serious enough to pose a danger, the county fire safety board has mailed a newsletter to all residents of the county, listing ways to detect a gas leak and encouraging householders to check for such signs.

Which of the following, if true, is the best criticism of the newsletter as a means of achieving the fire safety board's goals?

○ Many gas leaks have certain warning signs that cannot be detected during an investigation by a householder.

○ Once a gas leak is known to exist, the steps taken to eliminate such a hazard vary according to the type and location of the leak.

○ The newsletter was sent to all residents of the county, including those who maintain the standards of safety that preclude the possibility of a gas leak.

○ Gas leaks are more common in single-family homes than they are in apartments.

○ People who do not maintain minimal standards of safety are unlikely to inspect their homes for the signs of gas leaks.

10. Women make up a larger proportion of workers in the information services industry than they did 10 years ago. In 1985, only 7 percent of women in the workforce were employed in the information services industry, but in 1995, more than 16 percent of women in the workforce were employed in the information services industry.

To evaluate the truth of the argument above, it would be most useful to compare 1985 and 1995 with regard to which of the following characteristics?

○ The percentage of women in the workforce who were not employed in the information services industry

○ The percentage of women who are now retired, and who have formerly worked in the information services industry

○ The percentage of women who have been promoted to managerial positions within the information services industry

○ The percentage of men in the workforce who were employed in the information services industry

○ The percentage of men who will soon be eligible for employment in the information services industry

Reading Comprehension

Questions 1–3

Justice is the first virtue of social institutions, as truth is
of systems of thought. A theory, however elegant and
economical, must be rejected or revised if it is untrue.
Likewise, laws and institutions, no matter how efficient
5   and well arranged, must be reformed or abolished if they
are unjust. Each person possesses inviolability, founded
on justice, which even the welfare of society as a whole
cannot override. For this reason, justice denies that the
loss of freedom for some is made right by a greater good
10 shared by others. It does not allow that the sacrifices
imposed on a few are outweighed by the larger sum of
advantages enjoyed by many.

Therefore, in a just society the liberties of equal
citizenship are taken as settled; the rights secured by
15 justice are not subject to political bargaining or to the
calculus of social interests. The only thing that permits us
to acquiesce to an erroneous theory is the lack of a better
one; analogously, an injustice is tolerable only when it is
necessary to avoid an even greater injustice. As primary
20 virtues of human activities, truth and justice are
uncompromising.

These propositions seem to express our intuitive
conviction of the primacy of justice. One might inquire
whether these contentions or others similar to them are
25 sound, and if so, how they can be accounted for. To this
end, it is necessary to work out a theory of justice in
light of which these assertions can be interpreted and
assessed.

Begin by considering the role of principles of justice.
30 Assume that a society is a more or less self-sufficient
association of persons who, in their relations to one
another, recognize certain rules of conduct as
binding and who, for the most part, act in accordance
with them. Suppose further that these rules specify a
35 system of cooperation designed to advance the good of
those taking part in it. Then, although a society is a
cooperative venture for mutual advancement, it is
typically marked by a conflict as well as by an identity

of interests. There is an identity of interests since social
40 cooperation makes possible a better life for all than any
would have if each were to live solely by his own efforts.
There is a conflict of interests since persons are not
indifferent to how the greater benefits produced by their
collaborations are distributed, for in order to pursue their
45 ends they each prefer a larger to a lesser share.

A set of principles is required for choosing among the
various social arrangements that determine this division
of advantages and for underwriting an agreement on the
proper distributive shares. These principles are the
50 principles of social justice: they provide a way for
assigning rights and duties in the basic institutions of
society and they define the appropriate distribution of the
benefits and burdens of social cooperation.

1. It can be inferred from the passage that the
   author believes that one can permit the use of
   an imperfect theory of justice

   ○ under no circumstances, for to do so
      would violate the idea of justice

   ○ only if it would allow for the greater
      good of the society

   ○ only if a more just theory cannot be
      found

   ○ whenever it is agreed upon by a
      majority of the society

   ○ whenever it would effectively prevent
      certain injustices

2. According to the passage, a society is
   characterized by all of the following EXCEPT

   ○ self-sufficient individuals

   ○ a collaborative effort for common
      progress

   ○ an adherence to certain rules of
      behavior

   ○ a conflict of interest among
      individuals

   ○ a common interest in social
      cooperation

3. The author implies that, in order to ascertain whether convictions concerning the inherent nature of justice are valid, one must

○ determine the context in which they can be assessed

○ shed light on the role of the principles of justice

○ meet all of the requirements of a just society

○ account for the principle of justice in society

○ establish a theory of justice with which to evaluate them

Questions 4–6

One of the most studied senses is vision. Scientists have carefully unraveled the connections of brain cells in the visual system and have studied how they respond to light, so we have many clues about how the brain takes
5 visual images apart. What is particularly elusive, however, is how the brain puts the pieces back together, turning two-dimensional patterns of light on the retinas into our perception of the visual world. In one case, however, the perception of color, we are beginning to get a good idea
10 of how the brain operates.

Most people think that the balance of red, green, and blue light reflected from an object into the eye determines the object's color. It is easy to demonstrate that this notion is not true, however, simply by noting that
15 objects remain the same color in daylight, fluorescent light, and incandescent light, each of which contains a mix of wavelengths of light very different from the others. Edwin Land, inventor of the instant camera, has provided an explanation of this phenomenon in what he calls the
20 *retinex theory*, a term that combines "retina" and "cortex" to suggest that both parts of the visual system are involved in perceiving color.

Retinex theory proposes that the retina and the cortex cooperate to perform some complex computations on
25 the basis of light received from all areas within the visual landscape. A separate computation is carried out for each of three wavelengths of light that correspond to

what we normally think of as red, green, and blue; the wavelengths to which the three types of receptors in the
30   retina are most sensitive. According to the theory, the color we perceive at a particular location is determined by three numbers, computed by dividing the amount of light received from that location at each wavelength by a weighted average of the amount of light at that
35   wavelength received from all parts of the field of vision. The weighted average gives more weight to light coming from close to the location in question than to that coming from far away. The three numbers, coordinates in a color space of three dimensions, uniquely determine
40   the color we see, just as the three dimensions of physical space uniquely define the location of an object. Land has conducted a number of experiments showing that the numbers computed in this way correctly predict what color an observer will see under a number
45   of unusual lighting conditions.

This remarkable theory suggests that our visual systems evolved so that we see the colors of objects as the same, regardless of the mix of wavelengths of light falling on our retinas. Furthermore, this complex computation is
50   carried out virtually instantaneously without our even being aware of it.

4.   According to the passage, the proportions of red, green, and blue light reflected by an object cannot be the sole determinants of the object's color because

○   color information about three wavelengths is not sufficient to produce the full spectrum of possible colors

○   the perceived color of an object changes with the ambient lighting of the object's environment

○   the image of an object is formed not by light coming from the object itself, but from other parts of the field of vision

○   variations in the mix of wavelengths illuminating an object do not affect its color

○   this information varies according to the object's proximity to the viewer

5. The passage suggests that Edwin Land created the name *retinex* (line 20) for his optical theory in order to

○ distinguish his theory from rival theories of the retina's operation

○ indicate that both the retina and the cortex are involved in color perception

○ differentiate between the actions of the retina and the actions of the cortex

○ imply that properties ascribed to the retina actually belong to the cortex

○ indicate that the cortex and the retina work together in perceiving location

6. It can be inferred from the passage that if the balance of red, green, and blue light entering the eye determined color, the apparent color of an object could be expected to change if the object were moved

○ from a blue background to a bright yellow background

○ from a sunlit room to a room with fluorescent lights

○ to a different set of coordinates in physical space

○ close enough to take up the viewer's entire field of vision

○ to a new area in the viewer's visual landscape

In the early 1970s, a new system of organizing the growing acquisitions of corporations was introduced. Called the *growth/share matrix*, this tool seemed to operate on the most logical of assumptions: Corporations
5   should sell off their losing divisions as determined by the divisions' positions on the matrix, and retain and increase those divisions that the matrix considered successful.

According to the *Harvard Business Review*, the Boston Consulting Group (BCG) introduced the matrix in
10   response to corporations that had entered the heyday of acquisition and diversification of the 1960s and early 1970s, and subsequently faltered with the energy crisis of 1973. The matrix worked by ordering each division according to its position within its industry overall. Thus,
15   managers had a tool for understanding the relative success of those businesses with whose fields they were unfamiliar. Enthusiasm over the matrix and its simplicity and apparent logic obscured one of the problems inherent in the initial situation: the wide range of
20   acquisitions these corporations had purchased.

The matrix evaluated the performance of the divisions in terms of their competitiveness within their fields and their cash value, but failed to analyze the relationships among divisions that made up a corporation's holdings. For
25   instance, a corporation that owned a newspaper chain and a paper mill would be advised to consider more than just the relation of the paper mill's performance to that of other mills. Beyond this, the matrix underestimated the amount of debt a corporation could safely assume.
30   And finally, the matrix was unable to provide information regarding the corporation's ability to manage even those successes identified by the matrix.

Simply having a number of separately competitively successful companies does not ensure that companies
35   will be able to support their owners without proper management and understanding. Despite the clarity and effectiveness of the growth/share matrix as a tool for determining divisions' performance, it could not long compensate for the difficulties present in the initial
40   situation it sought to alleviate: that of corporations believing that their particular management styles would function effectively for any type of smaller business they might acquire.

7. Which of the following best describes the main idea of the passage?

○ The growth/share matrix was a failure as an acquisition research tool, and hurt many corporations.

○ The growth/share matrix, though eagerly embraced at first, could not completely solve the problems it sought to address.

○ Corporations that acquire holdings that are both overly diversified and unrelated will not succeed in the business world.

○ Management style should be of primary concern when a corporation is deciding which divisions to retain and which to divest.

○ No one corporate tool can ever compensate for a lack of management skills and well-thought-out acquisition planning.

8. According to the passage, all of the following were problems associated with corporations' reliance on the growth/share matrix EXCEPT

○ the overestimation by the matrix of the negative effect that debt might have on a corporation

○ not considering divisions' relation to one another within each corporation's holdings

○ the failure of the matrix to compensate for the lack of knowledge the corporations had about their own holdings

○ the matrix's inability to correctly order divisions within their overall industries

○ the matrix's lack of focus on a corporation's ability to manage its acquisitions

9. It can be inferred from the passage that the author suggests which of the following concerning some corporations during the energy crisis of 1973 ?

○ The troubles of these corporations were related to problems of conforming their management styles to their new holdings.

○ Lack of fuel led many companies to have trouble powering their acquisitions.

○ Corporations' reliance on the growth/share matrix led them to mismanage their holdings.

○ Overenthusiastic buying of smaller companies left many corporations unwieldy and difficult to manage.

○ Too little diversification forced companies to find a tool to estimate the relative success of companies with whose fields they were unfamiliar.

Answers and Explanations

Sentence Correction Drill Answer Key

1.	**E**	6.	**D**
2.	**B**	7.	**A**
3.	**E**	8.	**C**
4.	**A**	9.	**C**
5.	**B**	10.	**D**

Sentence Correction Drill Answers and Explanations

1. **E** Did you find the error in the sentence? It contains a parallel construction error. The sentence compares *the United States* to *the Prime Minister*. A secondary error is the misuse of *where*. Remember that *where* is for physical locations only.

   (A) No. The sentence contains an error, so get rid of this answer choice, as it is always identical to the underlined portion of the sentence.

   (B) No. This answer choice compares *the United States* to *the Prime Minister*.

   (C) No. This choice is not parallel—it compares *that of the United States* to *India*.

   (D) No. This answer choice compares *the United States* to *the Prime Minister*. Furthermore, it uses the word *where* instead of *in which*.

   (E) Yes. The stem sentence's problem is fixed, because the sentence parallels *in the United States* with *in India*. Additionally, the misuse of *where* is corrected.

2. **B** This sentence contains a comparison that's not parallel. The correct construction is *for women as well as for men*.

   (A) No. This is not parallel. Handguns are the most popular *for women*, and so they should be the most popular *for men*, too.

   (B) Yes. This sentence contains the correct idiom *as well as* and uses parallel construction to compare how popular handguns are *for women* and *for men*.

   (C) No. This choice is not parallel, and *and...too* is redundant.

   (D) No. This is not parallel. Also, *and...as well* is redundant.

   (E) No. This is not parallel, and *and also* is redundant.

3. **E** This sentence contains a pronoun error. *Team* is singular, so the underlined portion should read *it had*...All but one of the answer choices repeat the error.

(A) No. *Team* is singular, so the pronoun should be *it*, not *they*.

(B) No. *Team* is singular, so the pronoun should be *it*, not *their*. Also, this choice makes it sound as though the years had provisions.

(C) No. This contains the same pronoun error as the original sentence: *Team* is singular, so the pronoun should be *it*, not *they*.

(D) No. Pronoun error again—*Team* is singular, so the pronoun should be *it*, not *their*.

(E) Yes. This answer choice fixes the stem's pronoun problem by replacing the plural *they* with a singular *it*.

4. **A** This is a long sentence, but it has no apparent errors. Since you could not spot the error in the underlined portion of the sentence, you should have gone to each answer choice, and when you found an error there, eliminated it.

(A) Yes. This answer choice is long and a bit clunky, but it doesn't violate any rules.

(B) No. As written, the sentence says that *one reason* is *clustered next to each other*, which is a misplaced modifier.

(C) No. This choice contains the same misplaced modifier as (B). *Suggested by their customers* is another error—it is their behavior that suggests, not the customers themselves.

(D) No. Although it appears nearer to the end of the sentence rather than the beginning, *one reason* is modified by *if clustered next to each other*, which doesn't make sense. Furthermore, the sentence's subject, *the fact,* does not make sense with the sentence's verb, *is suggestive*. It is not the fact that is suggestive, but the customers' behavior.

(E) No. *The fact* does not suggest one reason the restaurants can succeed. Instead, consumers' behavior suggests one reason the restaurants can succeed. Also, the phrase *menus located in shopping malls* makes it sound as though the menus, rather than the restaurants, are located in shopping malls. And remember: GMAC hates *being*.

5. **B** This sentence contains a list—*raising, lowering*, and *a surge*—so you should expect an error in parallel construction. All the parts of the list must be the same part of speech for the list to be parallel. Since *a surge* is not underlined, you will need to find an answer choice that changes *raising* and *lowering* to nouns to match *a surge*.

    (A) No. Look for parallel construction. The other list item is *a surge* so we need *a raising* and *a lowering*.

    (B) Yes. This choice fixes the stem's parallel construction problem. The other list items are now *a raising, a lowering,* and *a surge*.

    (C) No. Although this choice fixes the stem's incorrect *raising* by making it *a raising*, it introduces a nonparallel phrase: *along with lowering fears about investing*.

    (D) No. This is not parallel—the nonunderlined portion of the sentence contains *a surge*, which is a noun, so we need nouns in the underlined portion of the list. Also, don't forget that ETS hates *being*.

    (E) No. We know ETS hates *being,* so we should eliminate this answer choice. It isn't parallel either. The other list item is *a surge* so we need *a raising* and *a lowering*. Also, for you grammar buffs, raising and lowering are transitive verbs, so they need a direct object (something that's raised or lowered).

6. **D** This sentence contains a verb tense error. When an event occurred in the past and is over, we use the simple past tense; in this case, *Act had a good chance of succeeding*. Look for the verbs at the ends of the answer choices. Eliminate (A) and (E) right away because the verbs are in the present tense. The sentence also contains an error in the use of the possessive: *colleagues of... Roosevelt's* is redundant. The correct usage is either *colleagues of...Roosevelt* or *Roosevelt's colleagues*.

    (A) No. This happened in the past, so *has* is wrong. Also, the possessive on *Roosevelt's* is redundant.

    (B) No. *Roosevelt's* is redundant.

    (C) No. *Roosevelt's* is redundant, and the verb tense in *have argued* is incorrect. The arguing occurred in the past, concluded in the past, and is not linked to any other event, so the verb should be simple past, *argued*.

    (D) Yes. This answer choice corrects the stem's incorrect *of... Roosevelt's*. Also, the two verbs are both in the simple past tense.

(E) No. This choice has a verb tense error. This event obviously happened in the past, yet the verb given here is the present tense *has*.

7. **A** If you don't see an error in the original sentence, go to Plan B—examine each of the answer choices to find an error and eliminate it.

  (A) Yes. This is direct and to the point. There is no error.

  (B) No. This is a verb tense error. We are dealing with the past, so the increase *was* 12 to 16 percent, not *is*.

  (C) No. The years are in the past, so it's incorrect to say that the average daily retail sales *have* increased. We need the simple past tense *increased*. Also, the idiom is used incorrectly—the increase should be expressed as *between 12 and 16 percent* or as *12 to 16 percent*.

  (D) No. This is the incorrect verb tense. We are dealing with the past, so it's incorrect to say that the increase *has* occurred.

  (E) No. It is too awkward to make the *increase* the subject of the sentence. The subject should be *sales*, and *increase* should be what happened to the sales.

8. **C** This sentence contains a problem in subject/verb agreement. The subject, *building,* is singular, so it needs a singular verb, *is known.* You can eliminate (A), (B), and (D).

  (A) No. The verb should be *is known as.*

  (B) No. This contains the same subject/verb agreement error as (A). Eliminate it.

  (C) Yes. A little clunky, but this choice fixes the stem's subject/verb problem.

  (D) No. This choice contains the original error of *are known.* Also, the first four words of this choice are very awkward. *Temperature* should not be used as an adjective to describe *spaces.*

  (E) No. This choice changes the meaning of the sentence. The interval spaces are not *supplied* with *temperatures.* Air flows through them. Eliminate this answer choice.

9. **C** The underlined portion of this sentence contains two errors: a subject/verb disagreement and a misused pronoun. The subject of the clause is *one-third*, which is singular, so it requires the singular verb *belongs*. *Who* should be *whom*. If you have trouble determining whether to use *who* or *whom*, restate the sentence substituting *he* or *him* for *who* or *whom*. In this sentence, *someone regards him as a neighbor*—since it's *him*, use *whom*. These two errors should allow you to quickly eliminate answer choices that contain one or both of them.

(A) No. *Belong* should be *belongs* to agree with *one-third* and *who* should be *whom*.

(B) No. This choice corrects the pronoun misuse but does not fix the subject/verb disagreement in *belong*.

(C) Yes. This choice uses the correct verb *belongs* and the correct pronoun *whom*.

(D) No. *Belong*s is correct, but *who* is not.

(E) No. Although this choice corrects the subject/verb disagreement and the pronoun misuse, it introduces a new error, *regards...to be*. The correct idiomatic expression is *regards ...as*.

10. **D** This sentence contains a subject/verb disagreement. *Each* is short for *each one* and is singular, so it calls for the singular verb *was*. You will quickly eliminate most of the answer choices if you focus on this error.

(A) No. This choice has an error in subject/verb agreement. *Each* is singular and needs a singular verb.

(B) No. Rearranging the sentence does not get rid of the subject/verb disagreement. The verb still needs to be *was* in order to agree with the subject *each*.

(C) No. Changing *each* to *every one* does not help. *Every one* is singular and needs the singular verb *was*.

(D) Yes. This choice is nearly identical to the original sentence except that it uses the correct verb *was*.

(E) No. The subject is still *each*, the verb is still *were*, and the sentence is still wrong. Plus, radically rearranging the sentence is rarely the solution to the grammar errors you'll see on the GMAT.

Arguments Drill Answer Key

1.	B	6.	B
2.	C	7.	A
3.	C	8.	B
4.	B	9.	E
5.	A	10.	D

Arguments Drill Answers and Explanations

1. **B** This argument asks you to support the editor's position, which hinges around her statement, *thus far*. Her point is that there may be patients who have taken the new drug and who have not yet shown side effects, but may in the future. She assumes that there are such patients, and the fact that patients have not shown side effects yet does not mean there aren't any. A good answer choice here will clearly establish that difference.
   - (A) No. You may have been tempted to pick this because it gives a side effect. However, this answer choice contradicts the editor's statement, in which no significant side effects are reported.
   - (B) Yes. The key in the editor's statement is *thus far*, which implies that side effects could still show up in the future, and this answer choice addresses that possibility.
   - (C) No. This is out of scope. The editor doesn't care about comparing this drug to others, just whether there are side effects of this drug.
   - (D) No. This is out of scope. The editor doesn't really care about the general state of hypertension in the United States.
   - (E) No. Both individual side effects and all hypertension drugs are out of scope.

2. **C** This is an inference question, so we need an answer choice we know to be true from the argument. All we know about is the ability of one particular computer program to detect counterfeit currency, and how it does so.
   - (A) No. We have no idea how expensive the program is, and *prohibitively* is extreme.
   - (B) No. Possibly, but nothing in the argument talks about consumer banks, so this is out of scope.

(C) Yes. This is the correct answer. The passage says that even the best counterfeiters can't hope to reproduce all facets of a nation's currency, and that the program contains extensive profiles of all major currencies. Even if you're inclined to argue that the passage doesn't say the program contains profiles of *all* techniques and components, it's still a better answer than any of the others.

(D) No. This may be true, but the information in the passage doesn't tell us how long development of the program took.

(E) No. This appears nowhere in the passage, and in fact contradicts the argument that this program works very well.

3. **C** We need to attack the assistant director's argument. He proposes to hire teachers who have *La Langue Facile* lesson plans instead of changing to a less time-intensive instructional tape series. If we can show that his plan would not have the desired result of allowing teachers to spend more time with their students, we will have weakened his argument.

(A) No. Class requirements and new educational standards are out of scope.

(B) No. If anything, this answer choice would strengthen the assistant director's argument, because it indicates that his plan may be somewhat easy to implement.

(C) Yes. The assistant director wants to hire teachers who already have *La Langue Facile* lesson plans because he assumes they will have more time to spend with students. But here we find out that those teachers will just have to use that lesson-planning time somewhere else. This weakens the assistant director's argument.

(D) No. Fluency test scores and students' performance are out of scope.

(E) No. This just tells us why switching to *Les Bons Mots* may not save time. Be careful. This answer choice weakens the *director's* point of view, not the assistant director's.

4. **B** Here we want to know about safety features, and whether they're important to buyers. To weaken the CEO's conclusion that safety features were not important, we need to show that consumers did consider safety to be important, or show another explanation for the consumers' decision.

(A) No. This is out of scope. We don't care who the buyers are; we need only to weaken the idea that safety features weren't important to those buyers.

(B) Yes. We have evidence that safety features are important to buyers; it's just that the buyers have a different opinion of what makes a vehicle safe.

(C) No. This doesn't explain the difference between this company's old and new models' performance.

(D) No. It doesn't matter to what age groups the car appeals. This is out of scope.

(E) No. Knowing that the price is the same does not help us weaken the argument. If we had learned the new model was cheaper, however, we would have had an alternate cause for the sales results, which would have been a good way to weaken the argument.

5. **A** This is a reasoning question, so pay attention to how the author constructs his argument. He takes a historical trend and uses it to predict the outcome of a specific event. As you read through the answer choices, simply ask yourself, "Did he do that?"

(A) Yes. The author based his conclusion about Tenon on the assumption that what has been true in the past (in an IPO, a company that seemed likely to generate profits saw an increase in their stock price) will be true for Tenon.

(B) No. There is no circular reasoning here.

(C) No. There is no confusion of cause and effect—potential profits cause an increase in stock price.

(D) No. There are no counterexamples given, so this answer choice is out of scope.

(E) No. There is no comparison made in the argument, so this cannot be the credited response.

6. **B** Resolve the Paradox: How can operating costs be lower when the new equipment is so expensive?

(A) No. This is out of scope. We are concerned with air-filtering equipment, not garments or facial filters.

(B) Yes. Here we are given an explanation of how operating costs could go down (the shutdowns, with their expense, are eliminated) even as the new equipment is present. The equipment actually forestalls additional costs.

(C) No. This tells us that operating costs went up, not how they went down.

(D) No. This answer choice also tells us about how operating costs went up, not how they went down.

(E) No. Though this answer choice does give some details about the new equipment, it doesn't tell us why operating costs could have gone down.

7. **A** Resolve the Paradox: How can the government subsidize diamond producers and still not experience an increase in net cost? (Note that the second part of the paradox is in the question, not in the argument.)

(A) Yes. Here we find out that the government collected less in taxes from diamond producers when prices were bad. Paying subsidies would make up for the operating losses, increase diamond producers' income, and increase taxes to the government, which would compensate for the subsidies.

(B) No. This doesn't help. If diamond production in other countries declined, then prices for diamonds would increase overall and the program would be unnecessary.

(C) No. This answer choice tells us the goal of the program is satisfied, but it doesn't tell us anything about the cost to the government. It speaks to only one side of the paradox.

(D) No. This answer choice doesn't talk about the overall effect that the subsidies would have on the government.

(E) No. This is irrelevant. The rules imposed on the diamond producers won't change the money the government pays them, and that's the issue we're interested in.

8. **B** This is an inference question, so the correct answer will be something you know from the argument.

(A) No. We have no information about the drugs' cost to the patient.

(B) Yes. If the companies can no longer place surcharges on more popular drugs, they will lose the sources of revenue that balance the losses from orphan drugs. They will have to find other revenue sources or lose money.

(C) No. The passage provides no information about generic drugs—it's out of scope.

(D) No. This is contradicted by the argument, which says there will be a constant percentage of profit allowed. So if drug costs are reduced, the profit should be commensurately reduced.

(E) No. There is no information in this argument about charitable organizations and offsetting of costs.

9. **E** This is a weaken question, so we need to attack the author's assumption that the newsletter will cause early detection of gas leak hazards. Since his assumption is a causal one, the best attack will either show that the newsletter will not cause early detection of gas leaks, or that something else will cause early detection of gas leaks, so the newsletter is not necessary.

(A) No. The nondetectable signs of gas leaks are out of scope. We are concerned only with the detectable warning signs of a gas leak.

(B) No. This answer choice focuses on what happens after detection, so it's out of scope. We're interested only in detection.

(C) No. This does not attack the causal assumption, so eliminate it.

(D) No. It doesn't matter what kind of dwelling is involved. It's out of scope.

(E) Yes. Here we learn that the newsletter probably won't cause early detection, because the people who are at risk won't check for leaks.

10. **D** This question asks what additional information we need to make the argument's conclusion true, so it's asking for an assumption. The author concludes that women make up a larger proportion of the workers in the information services industry based on his premise that a larger percentage of all women in the workforce are employed in this industry. In order for this conclusion to be true, we need to know that the corresponding percentage for men has shrunk, or that the increase in women in the information services sector is not due to growth across the entire workforce.

(A) No. Since we know that 7 percent of women in the workplace were in the information services industry, we already know that 93 percent were *not* in it, so this answer choice doesn't give us any new information.

(B) No. Retired women are out of scope.

(C) No. The specific positions of women in the industry are out of scope.

(D) Yes. If we know the percentage of male workers, we can tell whether the entire workforce has grown, or whether the corresponding percentage of men in the information services industry has shrunk.

(E) No. This is out of scope. We need to know what's happening now, not what will soon be happening.

Reading Comprehension Drill Answer Key

1. **C**   6. **B**
2. **A**   7. **B**
3. **E**   8. **D**
4. **D**   9. **A**
5. **B**

Reading Comprehension Drill Answers and Explanations

1. **C** This is an inference question so the answer to the question will be found in the passage. The subject of the question is the *use of an imperfect theory of justice* and the task is to find out what the *author believes* according to the passage. The second paragraph states that *an injustice is tolerable only when it is necessary to avoid an even greater injustice* so look for an answer choice that reflects this idea.

    (A) This is a reversal wrong answer as the passage actually states that there is a circumstance for the use of an imperfect theory of justice. Eliminate choice (A).

    (B) This is a recycled language wrong answer. The first paragraph uses the phrase *greater good* but not as a means to answer the question provided. Eliminate (B).

    (C) This is a good paraphrase of the passage which states injustice is only tolerable if a more just theory is not known. Keep choice (C).

    (D) This is a recycled language wrong answer. The first paragraph uses the phrasing *majority of society* but not as a reason to use an imperfect theory of justice. Eliminate (D).

    (E) This is a no such comparison answer as the passage does not compare the use of an imperfect theory to the prevention of other injustices. Eliminate (E).

2. **A** This is a retrieval question as evidenced by the presence of the phrase *According to the passage* in the question stem. The subject is a society, and the task is characterized by all of the following EXCEPT. The passage says that a society is *a more or less self-sufficient association of persons who...recognize certain rules of conduct as binding and...act in accordance with them.* It is also described as a system of cooperation designed to advance the good of those taking part in it. It is therefore a cooperative venture for mutual advancement even though it is typically marked by a conflict as well as by an identity of interests. The passage also mentions that social cooperation makes possible a better life for all. Find the answer choice that says something that is NOT reflected by one of these ideas.

   (A) The society is described as self-sufficient but not the persons, so keep choice (A).

   (B) The society is described as collaborative as it makes for a better life for all. Since this is how a society is described, eliminate (B).

   (C) Society is described as having rules of conduct that people act in accordance to, so eliminate choice (C).

   (D) This is a memory trap as there are conflicts of interest in a society that are mentioned in the passage, so eliminate choice (D).

   (E) Social cooperation is a memory trap from the passage that uses that terminology to describe a society, so eliminate choice (E).

3. **E** This is an inference question as evidenced by the phrase *implies that*. The subject is convictions concerning the inherent nature of justice, and the task is to determine what one must do in order to ascertain whether *convictions...are valid*. The passage says that, speaking of convictions, *it is necessary to work out a theory of justice in light of which these assertions can be interpreted and assessed.*

   (A) The word *assessed* is recycled language from the passage, but the context is not the item that needs to be developed according to the passage. The theory is, so eliminate choice (A).

   (B) *Shed light* is extreme language that is not a good paraphrase of the passage that says one must work out a theory. Eliminate (B).

(C) *Requirements of a just society* is a memory trap from the passage, as the majority of the passage is about that idea. However, it is not in context for this question so eliminate choice (C).

(D) *Principle of justice* is recycled language for the passage that is not pertinent to the answer for this question, so eliminate choice (D).

(E) This answer choice is a good paraphrase of the passage as this answer says one needs to establish a theory. Keep choice (E).

4. **D** This is a retrieval question. The subject is *the proportions of red, green, and blue light* and the task is to determine what the passage says about why they *cannot be the sole determinants of the object's color*. The passage says that *objects remain the same color in daylight, fluorescent light, and incandescent light, each of which contains a mix of wavelengths of light very different from the others* and so the *notion* of an object's color determines the perception of that color is *not true*.

(A) This is a reversal answer choice as the passage says that color information alone is not enough information to determine color, so eliminate (A).

(B) This is a reversal answer because the passage says that when lighting changes, the color of objects does not change, which is the cause of the stance that the notion in question is not true. Eliminate (B).

(C) This is a no such comparison answer as the passage does not seek to identify the *image* of the object. Eliminate (C).

(D) This is a good paraphrase of the passage as the passage does say that variations in the wavelengths around the object don't affect its color. Keep choice (D).

(E) This is a no such comparison answer as the passage does not seek to address anything about an object's *proximity to the viewer*.

5. **B** This is an inference question. The subject is *Edwin Land* and the task is to determine why he *created the name retinex for his optical theory*. The passage says that *the retinex theory...combines "retina" and "cortex" to suggest that both parts of the visual system are involved in perceiving color*.

(A) This is a no such comparison answer as the passage does not discuss *rival theories of the retina's operation* as why Edwin Land named his theory the retinex theory. Eliminate choice (A).

(B) This is a good paraphrase of the passage as the passage states that both parts of the visual system are involved in color perception. Keep choice (B).

(C) This is a no such comparison answer as the actions of the retina and cortex are not compared as a reason for the name of the theory. Eliminate (C).

(D) This is a reversal answer because the passage says that the two systems cooperate. Eliminate (D).

(E) This is a reversal answer choice because the retina and the cortex do work together but not to perceive location. Eliminate (E).

6. **B** This is an inference question. The subject is that if the *balance of red, green, and blue light entering the eye determined color* and the task is to determine which of the answer choices would be expected to happen to *the apparent color of an object…to change if the object were moved*. The passage states that color is not determined by red, green, and blue light because *objects remain the same color in daylight, fluorescent light, and incandescent light*. Since most people expect that light entering the eye causes the perception of color, the color of an object could be expected to change if the object were moved to a place with different light.

(A) This is reversal answer as the passage does not argue for this outcome. Eliminate (A).

(B) The change in light would cause the expected change in color. Keep choice (B).

(C) This is a no such comparison answer as the passage does not attempt to compare the object's physical location in space to its color. Eliminate (C).

(D) This is a no such comparison answer as the passage does not attempt to compare how close the object is in the viewer's field of vision to its color. Eliminate (D).

(E) This is a no such comparison answer as the passage does not attempt to compare where the object is located in the viewer's landscape to the color. Eliminate (E).

7. **B** This is a main idea question. The passage is about the *growth/share matrix* and the passage says that *Enthusiasm over the matrix and its simplicity and apparent logic obscured one of the problems inherent in the initial situation: the wide range of acquisitions these corporations had purchased*. Find an answer choice that reflects that idea.

(A) This is an extreme language answer choice. The growth/share matrix did not *fail* as an acquisition tool, according to the passage. Eliminate choice (A).

(B) This is a good paraphrase of the passage. The growth/share matrix was embraced but could not completely solve the problems. Keep choice (B).

(C) This is an extreme language answer choice. The passage does not argue that companies *will not succeed in the business world* if they have holdings that are *both overly diversified and unrelated*. Eliminate (C).

(D) This is a memory trap answer as the passage does mention management style as important, but this is not the main point of the passage. Eliminate (D).

(E) This is another extreme answer choice. The language *No one corporate tool can ever* is too extreme, and the reference to a lack of *management skills* is a memory trap. Both are cause to eliminate (E).

8. **D** This is a retrieval question. The subject is *problems associated with corporations' reliance on the growth/share matrix* and the task is to figure out which of the answer choices was not cited as one of the problems. The passage says that the *matrix failed to analyze the relationships among divisions that made up a corporation's holdings, underestimated the amount of debt a corporation could safely assume, and was unable to provide information regarding the corporation's ability to manage even those successes identified.* So eliminate any answer choices that are reflective of this idea.

(A) This answer choice is mentioned in the part of the passage that says the matrix *underestimated the amount of debt a corporation could safely assume*, so eliminate (A).

(B) This answer choice is also mentioned in the passage that says the *matrix failed to analyze the relationships among divisions that made up a corporation's holdings*, so eliminate (B).

(C) This is also reflected in the part of the passage that says the matrix was *unable to provide information regarding the corporation's ability to manage even those successes identified*, so eliminate (C).

(D) This is correct, as the passage states that *The matrix evaluated the performance of the divisions in terms of their competitiveness within their fields and their cash value.* So keep choice (D).

(E) This answer choice is similar to choice (C) and is reflected when the passage says the matrix *was unable to provide information regarding the corporation's ability to manage even those successes identified.* Eliminate choice (E).

9. **A** This is an inference question. The subject of the question is *some corporations during the energy crisis of 1973* and the task is to figure out which of the following the *author suggests.* The passage says that many companies faltered with the energy crisis of 1973, and the third paragraph lists all the reasons why they may have faltered. Find an answer choice that is reflective of the third paragraph.

(A) This is reflective of the section of paragraph three that says *the matrix was unable to provide information regarding the corporation's ability to manage even those successes identified by the matrix.* Keep choice (A).

(B) This answer choice is an appeal to outside knowledge, as the energy crisis could lead to thoughts of the need for *fuel,* but there is no indication of this in the passage, so eliminate choice (B).

(C) This is a recycled language answer with the reference to the *growth/share matrix.* While the third paragraph does mention this, it is mentioned as a tool for determining *divisions' performance,* and not related to the *energy crisis,* so eliminate choice (C).

(D) This is a memory trap as the passage does mention larger companies becoming difficult to manage, but this is not suggested about corporations during the energy crisis of 1973, so eliminate choice (D).

(E) This is another memory trap, as the passage does mention this is a problem, but this is not being suggested by the author about corporations during the energy crisis of 1973. Eliminate choice (E).

Math Drills

Problem Solving

1. If $\dfrac{0.036 \times 10^{a}}{0.09 \times 10^{b}} = 4 \times 10^{5}$, then $a - b =$

    ○ 7
    ○ 6
    ○ 5
    ○ 4
    ○ 3

2.

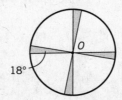

18°

To create a part for a certain piece of machinery, four equal-size wedge-shaped pieces are cut and removed from a circular piece of metal, as illustrated in the figure above. If the unshaded portion of the circle represents the material remaining after the pieces are removed, what percentage of the original circle remains?

○ 10
○ 20
○ 25
○ 60
○ 80

3. $\left(2+\sqrt{7}\right)\left(2-\sqrt{7}\right) =$

○ $-3 - 4\sqrt{7}$

○ -3

○ -1

○ $-4 - 4\sqrt{7}$

○ 11

4. The number of cells killed by a virus doubles every hour. If the number of cells killed was initially 10^3, what is the number of cells killed after eight hours have passed?

○ $8\left(10^3\right)$

○ $\left(10^3\right)\left(10^8\right)$

○ $2^8\left(10^3\right)$

○ $2^4\left(10^3\right)$

○ $2^8\left(10^8\right)$

5. For all numbers m and n, $m\Diamond n = \dfrac{m^2\left(m-n\right)}{n^2}$.

What is the value of $3\Diamond 2$?

○ $\dfrac{1}{2}$

○ $\dfrac{9}{4}$

○ $\dfrac{3}{2}$

○ 3

○ 9

6. In a certain egg-processing plant, every egg must be inspected, and is either accepted for processing or is rejected. For every 96 eggs accepted for processing, 4 eggs are rejected. If 12 additional eggs were accepted on one day, but the overall number of eggs inspected remained the same so that the ratio of accepted eggs to rejected eggs was 99 to 1, how many eggs does the plant process per day?

   ○ 100
   ○ 300
   ○ 400
   ○ 3,000
   ○ 4,000

7. In a 5-hour race, 6 cars consumed 480 gallons of gas among them. If all the cars consumed gas at the same constant rate, how much gas would be consumed by 7 such cars in an 8-hour race?

   ○ 560
   ○ 654.5
   ○ 768
   ○ 864
   ○ 896

8. If a golfer scores an average (arithmetic mean) of p points per round of golf for r rounds, and then scores q points in his next round, which of the following is an expression for the golfer's average score for the $\left(r + 1\right)$ rounds of golf?

   ○ $\dfrac{pr + q}{r + 1}$

   ○ $p\left(\dfrac{r + q}{r + 1}\right)$

   ○ $p + 2$
   ○ $p + 4$
   ○ $p + 12$

9. In the rectangular coordinate system, the line $2y - 3x = 14$ passes through each of the four quadrants EXCEPT

○ I
○ II
○ IV
○ I and IV
○ II and IV

10. Of the 140 moving trucks available to rent, 82 have air conditioning, 56 have automatic transmission, and 24 trucks have both air conditioning and automatic transmission. How many of the 140 trucks have neither air conditioning nor automatic transmission?

○ 4
○ 16
○ 26
○ 28
○ 32

11. On a certain day, a delivery driver must make 4 deliveries. He departs from the dispatch office and travels 14 miles due west to his first delivery. From there, his second delivery is 7 miles due north, and his third delivery is 9 miles due east of the location of his second delivery. His last delivery is 19 miles due south of his third. What is the distance, in miles, that the driver must travel to return to the dispatch office, if he travels in a straight line via the shortest route?

○ 33
○ 17
○ 13
○ 7
○ It cannot be determined from the information given.

12. A 6-sided die has 3 black sides and 3 white sides. If the die is thrown 4 times, what is the probability that, on at least one of the throws, the die will land with a black side up?

- $\frac{1}{16}$

- $\frac{3}{16}$

- $\frac{1}{2}$

- $\frac{9}{16}$

- $\frac{15}{16}$

13. A caterer must choose 3 canapés to serve from 12 possible selections. In how many possible combinations can he serve the 3 canapés?

- 220
- 440
- 660
- 1,100
- 1,320

14. A group of 10 coworkers has agreed to equally share the cost of a gift costing d dollars. If w of the coworkers later decide not to contribute, how much more must each of the remaining coworkers pay toward the gift?

○ $\dfrac{d}{10 - w}$

○ $\dfrac{d(w - 10)}{10w}$

○ $\dfrac{dw}{10(10 - w)}$

○ $\dfrac{10 - w}{d}$

○ $\dfrac{10dw}{10 - w}$

15. A merchant prices a television at 60 percent above wholesale. For a Presidents' Day sale, the merchant marks the television down by 25 percent. If he sells the television during the Presidents' Day sale, what percentage over the wholesale price will he have earned?

○ 75
○ 50
○ 35
○ 25
○ 20

16. A magazine stand owner sells cups of coffee, newspapers, and packs of gum. Compared to the number of cups of coffee he sells, he sells twice as many packs of gum, and three times as many newspapers. If he charges $1.25 for a cup of coffee, $0.50 for a newspaper, and $0.35 for a pack of gum, and sells no other items, which of the following could be the amount of his total gross sales on a given day?

   I. $345.00
  II. $58.65
 III. $22.15

- ○ I only
- ○ I and II only
- ○ I and III only
- ○ II and III only
- ○ I, II and III only

17. Ten strips of paper are numbered from 1 to 10 and placed in a bag. If three numbers are drawn from the bag at random, what is the probability that the sum of the numbers drawn will be odd?

- ○ $\dfrac{1}{12}$

- ○ $\dfrac{5}{36}$

- ○ $\dfrac{15}{36}$

- ○ $\dfrac{1}{2}$

- ○ $\dfrac{11}{18}$

18. Three actors and two dancers have individual auditions for a musical during the same afternoon. If no two actors are allowed to audition immediately following each other, in how many different orders could the five performers be seen?

- ○   3
- ○   6
- ○   12
- ○   24
- ○   120

19. If $a = 1{,}248$ and $b = 1{,}152$, what is the value of $(a^2 - b^2)^{\frac{1}{2}}$?

- ○   240
- ○   360
- ○   480
- ○   600
- ○   720

20. Working together, each at his or her own constant rate, Jeff and Ashley painted their apartment in 6 hours. Working at his constant rate, Jeff could have painted the whole apartment in 10 hours. How many hours would it have taken Ashley, working at her constant rate, to paint the apartment?

- ○   4
- ○   12
- ○   15
- ○   16
- ○   20

21. Which of the following fractions has a decimal equivalent that terminates?

- ⭘ $\dfrac{49}{224}$
- ⭘ $\dfrac{22}{189}$
- ⭘ $\dfrac{37}{196}$
- ⭘ $\dfrac{25}{513}$
- ⭘ $\dfrac{17}{175}$

22. Jaime has n comic books. He sells one-half of them and then gives one-third of the ones he has left to a friend. If he has 10 comic books left, how many did he have originally?

- ⭘ 30
- ⭘ 40
- ⭘ 60
- ⭘ 80
- ⭘ 90

23. Carol buys x widgets at a cost of y cents per widget. She packages them, q widgets per box, and sells them at a price of z dollars per box. What is the amount of profit, in dollars, that she makes on the sale (profit = sales revenue − cost)?

- ⭘ $100qz - xy$
- ⭘ $\dfrac{xz}{q} - \dfrac{xy}{100}$
- ⭘ $qz - \dfrac{xy}{100}$
- ⭘ $\dfrac{100z}{q} - xy$
- ⭘ $\dfrac{xz}{q} - xy$

24. If $2w + y = 47$, $3y + z = 112$, and $2w + 3z = 21$, what is the average (arithmetic mean) of w, y, and z ?

○ 15
○ 25
○ 50
○ 100
○ It cannot be determined from the information given.

25. Circle Q has radius r. Circle P has a radius that is 50% greater than r. In terms of r, what is the area of circle P ?

○ $\dfrac{\pi r^2}{2}$

○ $\dfrac{3\pi r^2}{2}$

○ $2\pi r^2$

○ $\dfrac{9\pi r^2}{4}$

○ $3\pi r^2$

Data Sufficiency

Directions: Data Sufficiency problems consist of a question and two statements, labeled (1) and (2), in which certain data are given. You have to decide whether the data given in the statements are <u>sufficient</u> for answering the question. Using the data given in the statements plus your knowledge of mathematics and everyday facts (such as the number of days in July or the meaning of *counterclockwise*), you are to fill in the oval

- ○ if statement (1) ALONE is sufficient, but statement (2) alone is not sufficient.
- ○ if statement (2) ALONE is sufficient, but statement (1) alone is not sufficient.
- ○ if BOTH statements TOGETHER are sufficient, but NEITHER statement ALONE is sufficient.
- ○ if EACH statement ALONE is sufficient.
- ○ if statements (1) and (2) TOGETHER are not sufficient.

1. If $2^x(7^y) = z$, what is the value of z ?

   (1) $x - y = 1$
   (2) $2^x = 8$

- ○ Statement (1) ALONE is sufficient, but statement (2) alone is not sufficient.
- ○ Statement (2) ALONE is sufficient, but statement (1) alone is not sufficient.
- ○ BOTH statements TOGETHER are sufficient, but NEITHER statement ALONE is sufficient.
- ○ EACH statement ALONE is sufficient.
- ○ Statements (1) and (2) TOGETHER are not sufficient.

2. In the Kennedy High School swim club, 120 members swim the backstroke or the crawl or both. If 30 of these members do not swim the backstroke, how many members swim both the crawl and the backstroke?

   (1) Of the 120 members, 72 do not swim the crawl.
   (2) A total of 48 members swim the crawl.

   ○ Statement (1) ALONE is sufficient, but statement (2) alone is not sufficient.
   ○ Statement (2) ALONE is sufficient, but statement (1) alone is not sufficient.
   ○ BOTH statements TOGETHER are sufficient, but NEITHER statement ALONE is sufficient.
   ○ EACH statement ALONE is sufficient.
   ○ Statements (1) and (2) TOGETHER are not sufficient.

3. If p and q are integers, is $p + q$ odd?

   (1) $\dfrac{p}{3}$ is not an odd integer.
   (2) $p - q$ is an even integer.

   ○ Statement (1) ALONE is sufficient, but statement (2) alone is not sufficient.
   ○ Statement (2) ALONE is sufficient, but statement (1) alone is not sufficient.
   ○ BOTH statements TOGETHER are sufficient, but NEITHER statement ALONE is sufficient.
   ○ EACH statement ALONE is sufficient.
   ○ Statements (1) and (2) TOGETHER are not sufficient.

4. At the beginning of last year, a furniture store had 75 armchairs in stock, which had cost the store $600 each. During the same year, the store purchased a number of additional armchairs. What is the total amount spent by the store on the armchairs it had in stock at the end of last year?

(1) Last year, the store purchased 30 armchairs for $500 each.

(2) Last year, the total revenue from the sale of armchairs was $16,500.

○ Statement (1) ALONE is sufficient, but statement (2) alone is not sufficient.

○ Statement (2) ALONE is sufficient, but statement (1) alone is not sufficient.

○ BOTH statements TOGETHER are sufficient, but NEITHER statement ALONE is sufficient.

○ EACH statement ALONE is sufficient.

○ Statements (1) and (2) TOGETHER are not sufficient.

5. What is the ratio of the number of boys to girls on the school bus?

(1) The number of boys is 5 less than twice the number of girls.

(2) The difference between the number of boys and the number of girls is 35.

○ Statement (1) ALONE is sufficient, but statement (2) alone is not sufficient.

○ Statement (2) ALONE is sufficient, but statement (1) alone is not sufficient.

○ BOTH statements TOGETHER are sufficient, but NEITHER statement ALONE is sufficient.

○ EACH statement ALONE is sufficient.

○ Statements (1) and (2) TOGETHER are not sufficient.

6. How long did it take Bob to complete the race?

    (1)   If Bob were $\frac{2}{3}$ faster, his time would have been 3 hours.

    (2)   Bob's average speed was 30 miles per hour.

    ○   Statement (1) ALONE is sufficient, but statement (2) alone is not sufficient.

    ○   Statement (2) ALONE is sufficient, but statement (1) alone is not sufficient.

    ○   BOTH statements TOGETHER are sufficient, but NEITHER statement ALONE is sufficient.

    ○   EACH statement ALONE is sufficient.

    ○   Statements (1) and (2) TOGETHER are not sufficient.

7.

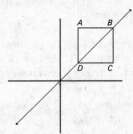

In the rectangular coordinate system above, is *ABCD* a square?

    (1)   Both Points *C* and *D* have *y*-coordinates of 3.

    (2) $\angle ABD = 45°$

    ○   Statement (1) ALONE is sufficient, but statement (2) alone is not sufficient.

    ○   Statement (2) ALONE is sufficient, but statement (1) alone is not sufficient.

    ○   BOTH statements TOGETHER are sufficient, but NEITHER statement ALONE is sufficient.

    ○   EACH statement ALONE is sufficient.

    ○   Statements (1) and (2) TOGETHER are not sufficient.

8. If $K = \dfrac{\dfrac{r}{3}}{\dfrac{p+2}{p^2-2p-r^2}}$, what is the value of K?

(1) $r = 2p$

(2) $p = 5$, and $2r - 2p = 2p$

○ Statement (1) ALONE is sufficient, but statement (2) alone is not sufficient.
○ Statement (2) ALONE is sufficient, but statement (1) alone is not sufficient.
○ BOTH statements TOGETHER are sufficient, but NEITHER statement ALONE is sufficient.
○ EACH statement ALONE is sufficient.
○ Statements (1) and (2) TOGETHER are not sufficient.

9. A drawer contains 12 socks, of which 8 are black and 4 are white. If 3 of the socks are removed, how many of the remaining socks are black?

(1) The remaining socks have a ratio of 2 black to 1 white.

(2) One of the first two socks removed is black.

○ Statement (1) ALONE is sufficient, but statement (2) alone is not sufficient.
○ Statement (2) ALONE is sufficient, but statement (1) alone is not sufficient.
○ BOTH statements TOGETHER are sufficient, but NEITHER statement ALONE is sufficient.
○ EACH statement ALONE is sufficient.
○ Statements (1) and (2) TOGETHER are not sufficient.

10.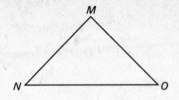

Is *MNO* a right triangle?

(1) $\overline{MN} = 2\sqrt{2}$

(2) $\angle MNO = \angle MON = \dfrac{1}{2} \angle OMN$

○ Statement (1) ALONE is sufficient, but statement (2) alone is not sufficient.

○ Statement (2) ALONE is sufficient, but statement (1) alone is not sufficient.

○ BOTH statements TOGETHER are sufficient, but NEITHER statement ALONE is sufficient.

○ EACH statement ALONE is sufficient.

○ Statements (1) and (2) TOGETHER are not sufficient.

11. Train A leaves the station at 5:00, and travels north at 50 miles per hour. If train B leaves the same station some time later, heading in the same direction as train A, at what time will train B overtake train A?

(1) Train B leaves the station at 6:00.

(2) Train A travels at $\dfrac{5}{6}$ the speed of train B.

○ Statement (1) ALONE is sufficient, but statement (2) alone is not sufficient.

○ Statement (2) ALONE is sufficient, but statement (1) alone is not sufficient.

○ BOTH statements TOGETHER are sufficient, but NEITHER statement ALONE is sufficient.

○ EACH statement ALONE is sufficient.

○ Statements (1) and (2) TOGETHER are not sufficient.

12. If e is a nonzero integer, is $\dfrac{1}{2^e}$ greater than or less than 1?

(1) $-e < 1$

(2) $e^2 > 0$

○ Statement (1) ALONE is sufficient, but statement (2) alone is not sufficient.

○ Statement (2) ALONE is sufficient, but statement (1) alone is not sufficient.

○ BOTH statements TOGETHER are sufficient, but NEITHER statement ALONE is sufficient.

○ EACH statement ALONE is sufficient.

○ Statements (1) and (2) TOGETHER are not sufficient.

13. What is the value of x ?

    (1)   x is the sum of two distinct prime numbers between 25 and 40.

    (2)   The sum of the distinct prime factors of x is 19.

○ Statement (1) ALONE is sufficient, but statement (2) alone is not sufficient.
○ Statement (2) ALONE is sufficient, but statement (1) alone is not sufficient.
○ BOTH statements TOGETHER are sufficient, but NEITHER statement ALONE is sufficient.
○ EACH statement ALONE is sufficient.
○ Statements (1) and (2) TOGETHER are not sufficient.

14. What is the value of x ?

    (1) $x(x-1) = 12$
    (2) $x(x+6) = -9$

○ Statement (1) ALONE is sufficient, but statement (2) alone is not sufficient.
○ Statement (2) ALONE is sufficient, but statement (1) alone is not sufficient.
○ BOTH statements TOGETHER are sufficient, but NEITHER statement ALONE is sufficient.
○ EACH statement ALONE is sufficient.
○ Statements (1) and (2) TOGETHER are not sufficient.

15. List *Q* contains 3 elements. What is the median of list *Q* ?

    (1)   The mean of list *Q* is 7.

    (2)   The mode of list *Q* is 5.

   ○   Statement (1) ALONE is sufficient, but statement (2) alone is not sufficient.

   ○   Statement (2) ALONE is sufficient, but statement (1) alone is not sufficient.

   ○   BOTH statements TOGETHER are sufficient, but NEITHER statement ALONE is sufficient.

   ○   EACH statement ALONE is sufficient.

   ○   Statements (1) and (2) TOGETHER are not sufficient.

16. Does more than 50% of the population of Lakeside subscribe to magazine *X* ?

    (1)   Lakeside has 1,000 residents.

    (2)   400 people in Lakeside subscribe to magazine *X*.

   ○   Statement (1) ALONE is sufficient, but statement (2) alone is not sufficient.

   ○   Statement (2) ALONE is sufficient, but statement (1) alone is not sufficient.

   ○   BOTH statements TOGETHER are sufficient, but NEITHER statement ALONE is sufficient.

   ○   EACH statement ALONE is sufficient.

   ○   Statements (1) and (2) TOGETHER are not sufficient.

17. Is $x + 1$ odd?

    (1) $2x + 5$ is odd.

    (2) $x + 6$ is odd.

    ○   Statement (1) ALONE is sufficient, but statement (2) alone is not sufficient.

    ○   Statement (2) ALONE is sufficient, but statement (1) alone is not sufficient.

    ○   BOTH statements TOGETHER are sufficient, but NEITHER statement ALONE is sufficient.

    ○   EACH statement ALONE is sufficient.

    ○   Statements (1) and (2) TOGETHER are not sufficient.

18. Does x have at least 3 prime factors?

    (1) $x = 5b$, where b is a positive integer.

    (2) $b = 2c$, where c is a positive integer.

    ○   Statement (1) ALONE is sufficient, but statement (2) alone is not sufficient.

    ○   Statement (2) ALONE is sufficient, but statement (1) alone is not sufficient.

    ○   BOTH statements TOGETHER are sufficient, but NEITHER statement ALONE is sufficient.

    ○   EACH statement ALONE is sufficient.

    ○   Statements (1) and (2) TOGETHER are not sufficient.

19. What is the area of rectangle *ABCD* ?

   (1) Side *B* is 7 units long.

   (2) The perimeter of rectangle *ABCD* is 20 units.

   ○ Statement (1) ALONE is sufficient, but statement (2) alone is not sufficient.

   ○ Statement (2) ALONE is sufficient, but statement (1) alone is not sufficient.

   ○ BOTH statements TOGETHER are sufficient, but NEITHER statement ALONE is sufficient.

   ○ EACH statement ALONE is sufficient.

   ○ Statements (1) and (2) TOGETHER are not sufficient.

20. What is the area of right triangle *ABC* ?

   (1) Side *B* is $7\sqrt{2}$ units long.

   (2) Triangle *ABC* is isosceles.

   ○ Statement (1) ALONE is sufficient, but statement (2) alone is not sufficient.

   ○ Statement (2) ALONE is sufficient, but statement (1) alone is not sufficient.

   ○ BOTH statements TOGETHER are sufficient, but NEITHER statement ALONE is sufficient.

   ○ EACH statement ALONE is sufficient.

   ○ Statements (1) and (2) TOGETHER are not sufficient.

Answers and Explanations

Problem Solving Drill Answer Key

1.	**B**	6.	**C**	11.	**C**	16.	**B**	21.	**A**
2.	**E**	7.	**E**	12.	**E**	17.	**D**	22.	**A**
3.	**B**	8.	**A**	13.	**A**	18.	**C**	23.	**B**
4.	**C**	9.	**C**	14.	**C**	19.	**C**	24.	**A**
5.	**B**	10.	**C**	15.	**E**	20.	**C**	25.	**D**

Problem Solving Drill
Answers and Explanations

1. **B** Break this problem into 2 different calculations. If $\dfrac{0.036 \times 10^a}{0.09 \times 10^b} = 4 \times 10^5$, then manipulate the problem into two different expressions. The two separate parts are $\dfrac{0.036}{0.09} \times \dfrac{10^a}{10^b}$. Solve these two parts independently to yield $0.4 \times 10^{a-b}$. Now multiply by 10 to move the decimal point, which results in $0.4 \times 10 \times \left(10^{a-b-1}\right) = 4 \times 10^{a-b-1}$. Plug this back into the original equation to find that $4 \times 10^{(a-b+1)} = 4 \times 10^5$. Solve for the variables in the exponents, so $a - b - 1 = 5$ and $a - b = 6$. The correct answer is choice (B).

2. **E** When you are asked to find a shaded portion of a circle, you have to figure out what fractional portion of the circle's 360° you're talking about. You know that the shaded portions of the circle have angles of 18° and that there are 4 of them. In essence, you are talking about $\left(\dfrac{18 \times 4}{360}\right)$, which is $\dfrac{72}{360}$, or $\dfrac{1}{5}$ of the circle. This leaves $\dfrac{4}{5}$, and that's 80 percent.

3. **B** You should use FOIL on a problem like this one.

$$\text{First: } 2 \times 2 = 4$$

$$\text{Outer: } 2 \times -\sqrt{7} = -2\sqrt{7}$$

$$\text{Inner: } 2 \times \sqrt{7} = 2\sqrt{7}$$

$$\text{Last: } \sqrt{7} \times -\sqrt{7} = -7$$

$$4 - 2\sqrt{7} + 2\sqrt{7} - 7 = 4 - 7 = -3$$

4. **C** If at the zero hour you have 1×10^3 virus cells, and the number doubles every hour, then after the first hour, you have 2×10^3. As you proceed, keep in mind what the answer choices look like—you don't need to multiply anything out. After the second hour you have $2^2 \times 10^3$, and so on. At the end of the eighth hour, you have $2^8 \times 10^3$ cells.

5. **B** It's a function problem, so everywhere you see an m in the original, put 3, and where you see an n, put 2.

$$3 \lozenge 2 = \frac{3^2(3-2)}{2^2} = \frac{9(1)}{4} = \frac{9}{4}$$

6. **C** The ratio of accepted to rejected eggs is 96:4. So for every 100 eggs, 4 are rejected and 96 are accepted. When 12 more eggs are accepted, the ratio shifts to 99 accepted and 1 rejected, which means that for every 100 eggs, 3 more are accepted and 3 fewer rejected. If, for every 100 eggs, 3 more are accepted, then for 12 more to be accepted using the same ratio, the plant must process 400 eggs ($3 \times 4 = 12$).

7. **E** This is a work problem in disguise. You must first determine the amount of gas one car consumes in one hour, so divide the total by the number of cars, and then the number of hours.

$$\frac{480}{6} = 80$$

$$\frac{80}{5} = 16$$

So each car consumes 16 gallons of gas per hour. In an 8-hour race, 7 cars would consume $16 \times 8 \times 7$, or 896 gallons.

8. **A** Plug in. If the golfer averages 90 (p) points per round, and he plays 4 (r) rounds, and then gets a 100 (q) on his next round, then his average score for the 5 games would look like this:

$$\text{Average} = \frac{\text{Total}}{\text{Number}}$$

$$\text{Average} = \frac{(90 \times 4) + 100}{4 + 1}$$

$$\text{Average} = \frac{(360) + 100}{5}$$

$$\text{Average} = \frac{460}{5} = 92$$

Carefully check all the answer choices; otherwise you might choose (D), $p + 2$. Choice (D) happens to be the answer for *this* set of numbers, but the real answer is choice (A). If you plug in and get two answer choices that work, simply plug in another set of numbers, and check only the two remaining answer choices.

9. **C** To graph a line, its equation must be in the form $y = mx + b$. Manipulate the equation you were given, $2y - 3x = 14$ until you have isolated y on one side of the equation.

$$2y - 3x = 14$$

$$2y = 14 + 3x$$

$$y = \frac{14 + 3x}{2}$$

$$y = \frac{14}{2} + \frac{3}{2}x$$

$$y = 7 + \frac{3}{2}x$$

$$y = \frac{3}{2}x + 7$$

So the slope of the line is $\frac{3}{2}$ and the y-intercept is 7. Sketch the coordinate grid on your scratch paper and plot the y-intercept at 7. Now plot the second point using the slope. Slope is $\frac{\text{rise}}{\text{run}}$, so count 3 up and 2 over to the right. (If the slope were negative, you would count 2 over to the left). Connect the points and draw your line.

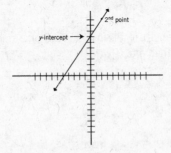

Your line passes through Quadrants I, II, and III, but not IV.

10. **C** This is a group problem, so use the formula
Total = Group 1 + Group 2 – Both + Neither

The total is 140, Group 1 is trucks with air conditioning (82), Group 2 is trucks with automatic transmission (56), and 24 trucks have both. Plug in what you know and solve for "Neither":

$$140 = 82 + 56 - 24 + \textit{Neither}$$

$$140 = 114 + \textit{Neither}$$

$$140 - 114 = \textit{Neither}$$

$$26 = \textit{Neither}$$

11. **C** When you are given no diagram, go ahead and draw one. To get from the last stop back to the dispatch office, the shortest route is a diagonal line, as shown in the diagram below. The diagonal line is also the hypotenuse of a right triangle, and the measurements of the two sides of that triangle are 5 and 12.

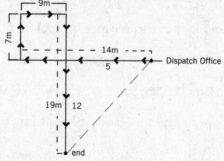

To find the length of the hypotenuse of a right triangle, use the Pythagorean theorem.

$$a^2 + b^2 = c^2$$

$$5^2 + 12^2 = c^2$$

$$25 + 144 = c^2$$

$$169 = c^2$$

$$\sqrt{169} = c$$

$$13 = c$$

So the distance is 13 miles.

12. **E** The probability of the die landing with a black side up on any one throw is $\frac{1}{2}$. The question asks for the probability that the die will land black side up on at least 1 out of 4 throws. This represents a lot of combinations.

It is quicker to think of it this way—the only outcome in which the die is *not* black side up at least once out of 4 throws is when all 4 throws are white. The probability of all 4 throws turning up white is $\frac{1}{16}$. You calculate this by multiplying the probabilities of each throw.

$$\frac{1}{2} \times \frac{1}{2} \times \frac{1}{2} \times \frac{1}{2} = \frac{1}{16}$$

If the probability that the die will *not* turn up black at least once is $\frac{1}{16}$, then in all the other outcomes, the die turns up black at least once. The total of all outcomes is always 1, so subtract the likelihood that black *won't* turn up from all the outcomes:

$$1 - \frac{1}{16} = \frac{15}{16}$$

So the probability that black will turn up on at least 1 of the 4 throws is $\frac{15}{16}$.

13. **A** This is a combination problem—one in which order does not matter. Use the formula $C = \dfrac{n!}{r!(n-r)!}$, in which n is the total number of things you're choosing from and r is the number you're choosing.

$$n = 12 \text{ and } r = 3$$
$$C = \frac{12!}{3!(12-3)!}$$
$$C = \frac{12!}{3!(9!)}$$

At this point, start reducing.

$$C = \frac{12 \times 11 \times 10}{3 \times 2 \times 1} = 2 \times 11 \times 10 = 220$$

If you erroneously used the formula for permutations, you would get 1,320. Notice that 1,320 is one of the choices.

14. **C** This is a classic Plugging In problem. Try using 100 for the cost of the gift and 2 for the number of coworkers who drop out. If 8 coworkers split the cost of the gift, it costs them each $12.50, which is $2.50 more than they had originally planned to pay.

Plug the same numbers into the answer choices, and you'll find (C) works. If you chose (A), that's the total amount each now pays, and the question wants only the increased amount.

15. **E** This is also a Plugging In problem—your answer choices are all percentages, so they are really variables. Use $100 for the whole-sale price of the television. The merchant marks it up 60 percent, or $60, which makes the price $160. He then reduces that price by 25 percent. 25 percent of $160 is $40, which makes the Presidents' Day sale price $120. The merchant makes $20 on the sale, which is 20 percent of the wholesale price.

16. **B** The smallest number of items would be 1 cup of coffee, 3 news-papers, and 2 packs of gum, for a total of $(1.25 + 1.50 + .70) =$ $3.45. Since all possible totals must be positive integer multiples of $3.45, $345 is possible since $345.00 = 3.45×100, and $58.65 is possible since $58.65 = 3.45×17. $22.15 is not possible, since $22.15 divided by $3.45 is not an integer. Thus, choices I and II are the only ones that work, so the answer is (B).

17. **D** There are two possible scenarios: All three numbers could be odd. The probability of this happening is $\frac{5}{10} \times \frac{4}{9} \times \frac{3}{8} = \frac{1}{12}$. In addition, one could be odd, and the other two could be even. Say that the first number is odd. Then this probability is $\frac{5}{10} \times \frac{5}{9} \times \frac{4}{8} = \frac{5}{36}$. But any one of the three numbers could be odd, so we should multiply the probability by three to account for the three different situations. This gives us $3 \times \frac{5}{36} = \frac{15}{36}$, and adding the first scenario to that gives us $\frac{15}{36} + \frac{1}{12} = \frac{15}{36} + \frac{3}{36} = \frac{18}{36} = \frac{1}{2}$.

18. **C** Since no two actors can audition back-to-back, the order must be ADADA. Now take each letter one at a time. There are three actors, so there are three possible choices for the first A, then two for the second A, and only one for the third A. There are only two possibilities for the first D, and only one for the second D. In ADADA order, then, there are $3 \times 2 \times 2 \times 1 \times 1 = 12$ possible orderings.

19. **C** This would be easy with a calculator, but you don't have one. Instead, remember to factor the difference of squares squares as $(a + b)(a - b)$. Then we're looking for the value of $(1{,}248 + 1{,}152)(1{,}248 - 1{,}152) = (2{,}400 \times 96)^{\frac{1}{2}}$.

Factoring further yields

$(100 \times 24 \times 96)^{\frac{1}{2}} = (100 \times 4 \times 6 \times 16 \times 6)^{\frac{1}{2}} = 10 \times 2 \times 6 \times 4 = 480$.

(*Note:* The exponent 1/2 is the same as square root.)

20. **C** Plug in your own number for the total amount of work. Remember to use multiples of the numbers in the problem, so try $6 \times 10 = 60$. Use this formula: rate $\times$ time = amount. If there are 60 walls to be painted, then working together they can paint 60 walls in 6 hours, or 10 walls/hour. Jeff working alone can paint 60 walls in 10 hours, or 6 walls/hour. Remember that you can add rates, so Ashley's solo rate plus Jeff's solo rate must equal their combined rate. So Ashley must paint at a rate of 4 walls/hour. If Ashley paints 60 walls at a rate of 4 walls/hour, she would have to work 15 hours to do the job by herself.

21. **A** Remember that a fraction has a terminating decimal equivalent as long as there isn't a factor of 7 or 3 in its fully reduced denominator. Of the answer choices, the only one that reduces away all 7's and 3's is (A). Factoring a 7 out of the numerator and the denominator yields $\dfrac{49}{224} = \dfrac{7 \times 7}{7 \times 32} = \dfrac{7}{32}$, which will terminate because 32 has only 2 as a prime factor.

22. **A** This is a good opportunity to plug in the answer choices. Start with 60. If he sells half, that leaves him with 30, and then he gives one-third, or 10, of those to a friend. That leaves him with 20, which doesn't equal 10. So not only is (C) wrong, but so are (D) and (E) since we need Jaime to be left with fewer than 20. We also know that n needs to be divisible by 6, so the answer can't be (B). Checking (A), we calculate that he gives away 15, and then 5 more to a friend, leaving Jaime with 10. That's the answer.

23. **B** Plug in your own numbers. Let's say Carol buys 100 widgets at $.30 each, so $x = 100$ and $y = .30$. Therefore, the cost of 100 widgets is $100 \times .30 = \$30.00$. Let's also say that she packages them at 5 per box and sells each box for $12.00, so $q = 5$ and $z = 12$. At 5 widgets per box, she will have 20 boxes (100 widgets ÷ 5 per box = 20 boxes). Therefore, her sales revenue is $12 \times 20 boxes = \$240$, and her profit is *sales revenue – cost*, or $240 – \$30 = \$210$. Now you can plug in to check your answer choices.

(A) is $100(5)(12) - (100)(30) = 3,000$, so it can't be right.

(B) is $\dfrac{100(12)}{5} - \dfrac{(100)(30)}{100} = 210$, which is what we want, but

be sure to check all the answer choices.

(C) is $(5)(12) - \dfrac{(100)(30)}{100} = 30$.

(D) is $\dfrac{100(12)}{5} - (100)(30) = -2,760$.

(E) is $\dfrac{100(12)}{5} - (100)(30) = -2,760$.

24. **A** To find the average, you must find the total of w, y, and z, and then divide by 3. Add the equations together to get $4w + 4y + 4z = 180$. Divide through by four, and you're left with $w + y + z = 45$. That's the total. Divide by 3, and the average is 15.

25. **D** Plug in. Pick 2 for r. The radius of P is 50% longer, or 3. The area of a circle with radius 3 is 9π. The only answer that matches when we plug in 2 for r is (D).

Data Sufficiency Drill Answer Key

1.	C	6.	A	11.	C	16.	C
2.	D	7.	E	12.	A	17.	B
3.	B	8.	B	13.	C	18.	E
4.	E	9.	A	14.	B	19.	C
5.	C	10.	B	15.	B	20.	E

Data Sufficiency Drill
Answers and Explanations

1. **C** Your first instinct here should be to think that statements (1) and (2) together are sufficient to determine the values of x and y, because as long as you have the same number of variables as you have equations, the data are sufficient. But in this case, one of the equations has an exponent, which means you need to work through the problem.

   So there's one equation in (1) and one in (2)—you have two equations. Using them together, you can define x and y, which then allows you to solve for z. Start with statement (1). It does not give you enough information, so write BCE on your scratch paper. Now take statement (2). If $2^x = 8$, then $x = 3$. Statement (2) alone is not sufficient, so cross off (B). You can take $x = 3$ and substitute it into the equation in statement (1), and that means that statement (1) and statement (2) together are sufficient to solve for x and y. With the values for x and y, you could determine the value of z.

2. **D** This is essentially a group problem, but nowhere in the problem do you have information about the "Neither" part of the group. This might lead you to hastily (and incorrectly) choose (E) as the answer. In fact, you have plenty of information.

   The question is asking about Group 1 (members who swim the backstroke), Group 2 (members who swim the crawl), and Both (members who swim both), so just use that part of the formula.

$$\text{Group 1} + \text{Group 2} - \text{Both} = 120$$

You know that 30 members do not swim the backstroke, which means that they swim only the crawl. Fill that in, so that you have

$$\text{Group 1} + 30 - \text{Both} = 120$$

Now proceed to the statements. You need only the numbers for either Group 1 or Both.

Statement (1) tells you that 72 members do not swim the crawl. These are the members who swim only the backstroke—Group 1. Statement (1) is sufficient, so write down AD. Statement (2) gives you the number of people who swim the crawl, which encompasses the 30 members in Group 2 plus the members who swim Both. This means there are 18 members who swim both strokes, and statement (2) alone is sufficient, so the answer is (D).

3. **B** On yes/no questions with variables, you have to plug into the statements twice. Try plugging in 6 and 2 for p and q the first time. Using statement (1), you find that $p = 6$ is not sufficient, so write down BCE. Plugging the same numbers, 6 and 2, into statement (2) works, so try them on the question. This is enough information, so statement (2) alone is sufficient this time.

Now choose another set of numbers to plug in. Try 0 and –2, and start with statement (2), because if it is still sufficient by itself, your answer is (B). And it is.

4. **E** To answer this question, you need to know how many armchairs the store sold and how many additional armchairs were purchased and what they cost. Statement (1) tells you the cost of the additional armchairs purchased, but is not sufficient, so write BCE. Statement (2) gives you a total without the number of armchairs it encompasses, so it is not sufficient. Cross off (B). Together the statements do not give you enough information.

5. **C** Two equations, two variables. Statement (1) can be rewritten as $b = 2g - 5$ and statement (2) can be written as $b - g = 35$. Alone, neither equation is sufficient, but together they are.

6. **A** For this question, you should use the distance formula *distance = rate × time*, or $d = r \times t$. Since the question asks "How long did it take Bob to complete the race," you know you're looking for time, or t. The problem is that you don't know d or r. So let's use the distance formula for the hypothetical situation in which Bob's time would be 3 hours if he were $\frac{2}{3}$ faster. That formula would look like this:

$$d = 1r + \frac{2}{3}r \times 3$$

$$d = 1\frac{2}{3}r \times 3$$

$$d = \frac{5}{3}r \times 3$$

$$d = \frac{15}{3}r$$

$$d = 5r$$

At this point you have two terms equal to d. Those terms are $r \times t$ and $5r$. If both of these terms are equal to d, then they're equal to each other:

$$r \times t = 5r$$

$$t = 5$$

Bob's time in the race was 5 hours. Statement (1) is sufficient to answer the question, so narrow your choices to (A) and (D).

Now look at statement (2). Knowing Bob's rate alone will not help you determine the time it took him to complete the race, so eliminate (D). The answer is (A).

7. **E** For a quadrilateral to be a square, it must have four equal sides and four equal angles of 90°. So you'll need to know the lengths of the sides and the angle measurements.

Redraw the diagram on your scratch paper, and label everything you know. Statement (1) tells you that points C and D have y-coordinates of 3, but this does not work alone, so write BCE. Statement (2) tells you that the angle formed by the diagonal is 45°, but this does not tell you the measurement of $\angle DBC$, or any other angle, for that matter. So statement (2) alone is not sufficient. Even taken together, statement (1) and statement (2) do not tell you the lengths of the sides or the measure of the angles of the quadrilateral, so the data are not sufficient.

8. **B** You need two equations, because you have two variables. Statement (1) gives you only one. But statement (2) gives you two equations, and from that information, you can determine the values of p and q (and therefore K, but don't waste your time with K—remember that you don't have to solve). So statement (2) alone is sufficient.

9. **A** This question looks like a probability question, but it is actually simpler than that. Start with statement (1). By removing 3 of the 12 socks, you have reduced the number of socks in the drawer to 9. Statement (1) tells you the socks remaining in the drawer have a ratio of 2 to 1, so you have 6 black and 3 white socks. This answers the question, and statement (1) is sufficient, so write down AD.

Statement (2) tells you one of the first 2 socks removed is black, but tells you nothing about what's left or what else you removed, so it is not sufficient. The answer is (A).

10. **B** Statement (1) tells you the length of the hypotenuse, and while it looks like a typical measurement of the hypotenuse of a right triangle, statement (1) is not sufficient to guarantee this is a right triangle. Write down BCE.

Statement (2) gives you all the information you need: The angles in a triangle add up to 180°, and you know the relationship of all three angles to each other. If you went ahead and solved using statement (2), you'd learn that the triangle has two 45° angles and one 90° angle. But why waste your time, when you know that statement (2) alone is sufficient?

11. **C** There are a couple of different ways to crack this problem, but perhaps the most straightforward is for you to just reason through it—no algebra necessary. Train A is chugging along at a leisurely 50 mph. In order for train B to overtake train A, it simply has to be travelling faster than 50 mph. We don't care how long it actually takes; *we care only whether we could figure out how long it takes, if we had to.*

Statement (1) tells you what time train B leaves the station. This does not tell us whether train B is faster than train A, so it is not sufficient. Write down BCE. Statement (2) tells us that train B is faster than train A, so statement (2) and statement (1) are sufficient—the answer is (C).

12. **A** First consider statement (1), which says $-e < 1$. There are two ways to approach this. First, if you remember how to simplify such statements, you will know that you can move the negative sign to the other side by switching the direction of the inequality, to get $e > -1$. Together with the fact that e is a nonzero integer, this tells us that e must be 1, 2, 3, 4, or some other, larger, whole number. We can plug a few of those values into the expression $\frac{1}{2^e}$ to see if the result is less than or greater than 1.

$$\frac{1}{2^1} = \frac{1}{2} \qquad\qquad \frac{1}{2^2} = \frac{1}{4} \qquad\qquad \frac{1}{2^3} = \frac{1}{8} \qquad\qquad \frac{1}{2^4} = \frac{1}{16}$$

Crash Course for the GMAT

All of these results are less than 1, and are getting smaller. Thus statement (1) is sufficient to answer the question; it tells us that $\frac{1}{2^e} < 1$. However, if you did not remember how to simplify $-e < 1$, you could instead just test various nonzero integers to see if they make it true. For example, you might try some negative numbers -1, -2, -3, and -4, and some positive numbers, 1, 2, 3, and 4. You would find that statement (1) accepts only the positive numbers, and none of the negatives. This would lead you to make an educated guess that you should pay attention only to positive integers, and then plug in a few, as described above.

Since statement (1) is sufficient, write down AD. Then, consider statement (2). Again, there are two approaches, based on how much you remember. For example, you may know that *any number at all* squared will be greater than or equal to zero. (Even if the number were negative, multiplying it by itself makes it positive.) Thus, statement (2), $e^2 > 0$, actually doesn't tell us anything we didn't already know; statement 2 still permits both negative and positive values of *e*. Some examples are below. However, if you didn't know that fact, you could still discover it just by testing a few negative and positive values, and seeing if those values make statement (2) true. For example, plug in 1, 2, -1, and -2, and find that all of them make statement (2) true.

$1^2 = 1 > 0 \qquad 2^2 = 4 > 0 \qquad (-1)^2 = 1 > 0 \qquad (-2)^2 = 4 > 0$

So we can try out these same values of e in $\dfrac{1}{2^e}$ to see if it comes out consistently greater than 1, consistently less than 1, or a mix.

$$\dfrac{1}{2^1} = \dfrac{1}{2} < 1 \qquad \dfrac{1}{2^2} = \dfrac{1}{4} < 1 \qquad \dfrac{1}{2^{-1}} = 2 > 1 \qquad \dfrac{1}{2^{-2}} = 4 > 1$$

Since some are less than 1 and some are greater than 1, we cannot say that either $\dfrac{1}{2^e} < 1$ or $\dfrac{1}{2^e} > 1$ happens consistently for every value of e. Therefore, statement (2) is *not* sufficient to answer the question. So the final answer for this data sufficiency question is (A).

13. **C** Looking at statement (1) alone, you can determine that there are three distinct prime numbers between 25 and 40: 29, 31, and 37. Thus, x could be 60, 66, or 68. So narrow your choices to BCE. Statement (2), by itself, would be satisfied by an x of 34 or 165, among others, so we cross out B. Looking at the two together, only 68 yields prime factors that sum to 19, so the best answer is (C).

14. **B** Expanding statement (1) results in $x^2 - x - 12 = 0$. Factoring that gives $(x - 4)(x + 3) = 0$, so $x = 4$ or $x = -3$ so you can narrow your choice to BCE. The second statement, however, factors into $(x + 3)^2 = 0$. Since the only solution to this statement is $x = -3$, the correct answer is (B).

15. **B** The first statement alone is insufficient. The lists (4, 5, 12) and (7, 7, 7) both have mean 7, but different medians. Narrow the choices to BCE. The second statement alone is sufficient. If the element 5 occurs most often, it must occur at least twice. If it occurs at least twice, is must be the median of the list. The answer is (B).

Crash Course for the GMAT

16. **C** Statement (1) doesn't give enough information, so narrow the choices to BCE. Statement (2) by itself doesn't tell enough either, so cross out (B). Taking both together, you find that less than 50 percent of the population subscribes to magazine X, which is enough to answer the question (and the answer happens to be "no").

17. **B** Start with statement (1). Try $x = 1$. Then $2x + 5 = 7$, which is odd, so try $x = 1$ with the original question. $x + 1 = 2$, which is even, so the answer to the question is "no." Does it always have to be "no"? Let's try $x = 2$, still in statement (1). That makes $2x + 5 = 9$. which is odd, so return to the original question with $x = 2$. Now, $x + 1 = 3$, which is odd, so the answer is "yes." Since sometimes the answer is "yes" and sometimes "no," the fact that $2x + 5$ is odd is not enough information to tell whether $x + 1$ is odd. Narrow the answers to BCE. Now do the same thing with statement (2). Try $x = 1$ again, which makes $x + 6$ odd. You already know that when $x = 1$, the answer to the original question is "no." Does it always have to be "no"? Try $x = 2$ with statement (2). $x + 6 = 8$, which is even, so you can't use $x = 2$. In fact, a little analysis or trial-and-error shows that only odd x's satisfy statement (2). This means that $x + 1$ will always be even, and the answer to the question will always be "no." Therefore, the correct answer is (B).

18. **E** Statement (1) indicates that x has at least one prime factor, 5. Therefore, narrow your choices to BCE. Statement (2) says nothing about x. Cross out (B). Taking them together, you know x has at least two prime factors, 5 and 2, but since c might equal 1, you don't know whether it has a third or not.

19. **C** The area of a rectangle equals length times width. Statement (1) doesn't provide enough information to determine the area, so narrow your choices to BCE. There's no direct relationship between the area of a rectangle and its perimeter, so cross out (B). Together, though, you know that two opposite sides must account for 14 of the 20 units, leaving 6 for the other two sides. Therefore, the width must be 3 units, and you can now calculate the area.

20. **E** The area of a triangle is $\frac{1}{2}bh$. Statement (1) gives only one side, so it can't be sufficient. Narrow your choices to BCE. Statement (2) says that triangle ABC is half of a square, but nothing else, so cross out (B). Now look at them together. Although statement (2) says that the sides of ABC have specific ratios, you don't know whether $7\sqrt{2}$ is the hypotenuse or one of the two equal legs, so you still don't have enough information to determine the area.